REGIONAL AND LOCAL ECONOMIC ANALYSIS FOR PRACTITIONERS

REGIONAL and LOCAL ECONOMIC ANALYSIS
FOR
PRACTITIONERS

New and Expanded Edition

Avrom Bendavid-Val

PRAEGER

PRAEGER SPECIAL STUDIES • PRAEGER SCIENTIFIC

088752

Library of Congress Cataloging in Publication Data

Bendavid-Val, Avrom.
　　Regional and local economic analysis for practioners.

　　Rev. ed. of: Regional economic analysis for practi-
tioners. Rev. ed. 1974.
　　Bibliography: p.
　　Includes index.
　　1. Regional economics. 2. Economic zoning. I. Title.
HT391.B38 1983　　　　338.9　　　　82-16695
ISBN 0-03-062912-8
ISBN 0-03-062913-6 (pbk.)

Published in 1983 by Praeger Publishers
CBS Educational and Professional Publishing
a Division of CBS Inc.
521 Fifth Avenue, New York, New York 10175 U.S.A.

© 1983 by Praeger Publishers

3456789　　　052　　　987654321

Printed in the United States of America

For Leah,
Who must never let June go by,
And for
Naftali, Ronnit, and Oren

CONTENTS

LIST OF TABLES

LIST OF FIGURES

PREFACE

In the early 1970s I published a book, Regional Economic Analysis for Practitioners, that now, ten years later, has given rise to this one. It was an attempt at simplified presentations of the more common and most widely useful descriptive methods of regional economic analysis. It was aimed at practitioners who needed to understand and use the analytical tools but who did not have a solid grounding in mathematics or economics. It stressed the pliability of the methods and encouraged practitioners to exercise creativity in molding them into forms suitable for application in the particular regions and working situations in which they found themselves. The style and format were designed to enable the book to serve both for purposes of independent or classroom study and as a working reference.

Quite a body of experience with the book in a wide variety of learning and working environments has now accumulated. I have had the personal pleasure of teaching in about 15 different programs and courses that used the book as a basic text in industrialized and non-industrialized capitalist and socialist countries, and I have visited planning projects in equally diverse contexts where the book was being used as a reference. To me, working with Regional Economic Analysis for Practitioners has confirmed the two basic premises on which it was written, namely: (1) that there is a need for literature in the field of regional-development planning that collects, selects, organizes, and spreads existing knowledge effectively, a need no less worthy or urgent than the need for new knowledge; and (2) that the worldwide usefulness of such a book is enhanced by presenting the material in a manner that stresses basic principles and is fairly independent of place-specific circumstances such as the particular types of data available.

In the present book, which incorporates and builds on the first, the basic style, format, and approach are preserved. This will disappoint those users of the earlier book who complained that they needed guidance in obtaining data, wanted more detailed discussions of the methods of analysis, or yearned for case studies of applications. Those things are important, but this book, meant to be a broad introduction, is not the place for them. Other literature, a portion of which is listed in the Bibliography, should be consulted by readers who want to know more.

But the working experience with Regional Economic Analysis for Practitioners over the years has also confirmed the need for some changes. That book was written with a certain regional-planning

frame of reference in mind. In the intervening ten years there has been
an increasing interest in regional-development planning and an associated proliferation of courses and programs in the subject. Yet there
is no evidence to suggest that there has been a significant increase in
the amount of regional planning, in the traditional sense, going on.
What has happened, it appears to me, is that there has been a growing
awareness that the tools and concepts of regional analysis and development planning have applications in a wide variety of situations, including rural, local, district, county, multicounty, provincial, and state
planning. All you really need is an open economy and some concern
with the spatial distribution of economic activity. Virtually any subnational area will do. So the present book was prepared with a broader
body of users and working situations in mind, and that is reflected in
some minor and major changes from the first book.

  Regional and Local Economic Analysis for Practitioners has
been expanded and divided into three parts. Part I contains a much
more extensive introductory chapter that provides a review of some
of the basic economic concepts behind the methods of regional analysis. It also introduces some aspects of the development context
within which the methods might be used.

  Part II encompasses Chapters 2-7, which present the methods
of regional economic analysis. These chapters cover the same general ground as did their counterparts in the first book, though they
have been revised, improved, and in some cases expanded. These
chapters remain the heart of the book. Each of the chapters in Part II
is followed by a set of exercises, designed as learning aids rather
than for testing purposes. An appendix has been added that provides solutions to some of the exercises.

  Part III, containing material absent from the first book, provides information concerning the planning contexts in which the
methods might be used. Chapter 8 briefly illustrates analysis for
development planning that makes use of the three methods of social
accounting covered in earlier chapters. Chapter 9 responds to a
growing need for limited approaches to regional and local analysis
and planning that can serve as initial bases upon which full-fledged
development-planning processes can be built. Chapter 10 deals with
cost-benefit analysis; it is meant both for project planners who need
to introduce a broader perspective into their analyses and for gen-
eral-development planners who need to understand the kinds of issues
with which project planners must grapple. Chapter 11 describes the
general planning process applicable at any administrative level, and
it lays out some of the considerations in adapting that general process
to a particular regional or local planning situation. All four chapters
in Part III follow the approach taken with regard to the methods of
analysis in Part II: the essence of the subject is given, and the reader
is encouraged to elaborate upon it in accordance with needs.

There is a burgeoning literature in subjects related to <u>Regional</u> <u>and Local Economic Analysis for Practitioners</u>, and I have been fairly selective in the books I have included in the Bibliography at the end of the book. The selections do not always represent the latest litera- ture, but rather what I believe will be most useful to practitioners. The book portion of the Bibliography is organized in sections cor- responding to Parts I, II, and III of the text. To stay abreast of cur- rent literature, the reader is referred to book lists and reviews ap- pearing in the final section (periodicals) of the Bibliography.

The Index shows the locations of important terms or concepts the first time they appear in connection with a particular discussion.

The field of regional-development planning grows richer in con- tent day by day. It has reflected the evolutionary pattern of related planning fields, such as national development planning, urban plan- ning, transportation planning, and environmental planning. In earlier days planning was viewed as a technical exercise. Indeed, some books on planning contained nothing more than tools of technical analysis. Experience has taught most development practitioners that planning is above all a process, and one that cannot be divorced from imple- mentation and management—that is, from the development process itself.

The reader who masters the material in this book will command the rudiments of certain concepts, theories, approaches, and espe- cially, methods of economic analysis useful in a regional or local development-planning context. The student or practitioner who wants to do justice to the field will have to be concerned as well with re- gional delineation, project identification and evaluation, resource analysis, unconventional socioeconomic analysis techniques, survey methods, basic statistical analysis, institutional frameworks for planning and development, program development and budgeting, par- ticipation techniques, demographic analysis, spatial analysis, and much more. Many readers will be less interested in doing justice to the field than in simply gaining a basic grasp of the subjects covered in the book. But they, too, should not lose sight of the fact that they are selecting the knowledge they most urgently need from a field that is vast and varied.

<u>Regional and Local Economic Analysis for Practitioners</u> began with the idea of a modest revision of the first book. Readers or users who want no more than that need not bother with Part III. Part III has been added in recognition of the fact that, powerful as the methods of analysis are, they are nothing outside a development-planning pro- cess through which people in regions and local areas attempt to shape their own destinies. In this book I hope to have done a better job of explaining the analytical methods and to have increased their useful- ness in the hands of analysts by linking them more closely to social decision-making processes.

ACKNOWLEDGMENTS

My thanks to Benita Anderson, for her help in preparing the manuscript, and to editor John Lambert and copyeditor Debbie Schoenholz. I am grateful to Eric Chetwynd, Jocken Eigen, John Friedmann, Jos Hilhorst, Chris Macie, Om Mathur, Edgar Owens, Christian Remy, Jorge Sapoznikow, Raanan Weitz, and Harold Williams for their observations and suggestions, and for opportunities they provided to test and refine material in this book.

PART I

THE ECONOMIC AND
DEVELOPMENT
CONTEXT

1

ASPECTS OF REGIONAL AND LOCAL ECONOMICS AND DEVELOPMENT

While the material in the following chapters comes mostly from the field of regional economic analysis, it has direct applications at virtually any subnational level. For purposes of this book a region can be thought of as a "subnational area with at least one urban place and an associated hinterland, an area that is part of a larger system and in which economic relationships over its internal space are an economic development concern." Regional planners in the traditional sense will be joined by rural planners, district and county planners, provincial and state planners, and urban planners in making use of the methods of regional analysis. In what follows the reader is reminded from time to time that this is the case by referring to a "region or local area." But even when the term region stands alone it should be understood as a generic term for a subnational area in which efforts to analyze, plan, implement, and manage economic development activity are being undertaken.

FROM NATIONAL TO REGIONAL ECONOMICS

Regional economics leans very heavily on the theories and tools of analysis developed for national economics. Making good use of the methods of regional economic analysis, however, requires an appreciation for the points of divergence between the economies of regions and the economies of nations.

We know, for example, that economic trade between nations tends to come about when, because of absolute or comparative advantages, both parties to the trade will gain from the exchange. A country may have production advantages that result from natural resource endowments, unique human or institutional resources, stra-

3

tegic locational features, or other special economic resources. The greater the advantages in some area of production, the more profitable will be specialization and trade, and generally, the greater will be the volume of trade.

These notions can serve as a foundation for understanding interregional trade as well as international trade. Yet, we know by experience or intuition that in most cases external trade plays a much greater role in the economy of a region or local area than in the economy of a nation. Why is this? What are the barriers to trade among nations that do not exist, or are not as serious, at the regional level?

In the first place, distances between national trading partners, and therefore the transportation costs associated with trade, are generally greater among countries than among regions trading within the same country. Defense and political considerations not uncommonly encourage countries to maintain production capabilities in certain commodities that might be purchased more cheaply in the international marketplace. National full-employment policies, cultural differences, xenophobia, balance-of-payments and exchange-rate problems, administrative red tape, and other trade-inhibiting factors found at the national level are generally absent or much less intense at the level of trade between subnational regions. Moreover, a nation has the legal tools—tariffs, quotas, and other institutional devices—to enforce a restriction of trade when it deems this to be in its best interests. These tools are generally unavailable to regions or local areas. With fewer natural and institutional barriers, regions or local areas tend to specialize and trade to a much greater degree than nations.

But not only goods flow more freely across interregional borders than across international borders; factors of production that are not fixed in place by nature—capital, labor, ideas, and techniques—also flow more freely. All this gives the regional economy a greater quality of general openness than is usually found at the level of the national economy.

What are the economic implications of the general openness that characterizes a regional or local economy? There are many. Again, they can begin to be understood by starting with what is known about the economies of nations.

Take, for example, what is known about national income determination. The conventional commodity-market model of the national economy holds that gross national product (GNP) is the sum of four components: domestic consumption spending, private domestic investment spending, domestic government spending, and net exports (exports minus imports). When there is an increase in any of these components, national product and income increase. Part of the in-

TABLE 1.1

Numerical Example of Income Multiplication

Example: Increase in domestic investment spending of Mu. 100. Assume total leakages (taxes, imports, savings, and so on)
amount to 40 percent.

Round	Amount Spent	Amount That Leaks Out
1st	Mu. 100	Mu. 40
2nd	60	24
3rd	36	14
4th	22	9
5th	13	5
6th	8	3
7th	5	2
8th	3	1
9th	2	.
.	.	.
.	.	.
.	.	.
Total	Mu. 250	Mu. 100

Mu. = monetary units

crease in income is spent again by those who receive it, generating
a further increase, which is again partly respent, and so on, round
after round. The reason only part of the increase in income is spent
in each round is because part leaks out of the spending stream into
taxes, purchases of imports, savings, and other leakages that do
not result in additional current domestic income. In each round there
is less spending and less new income generated than in the round
before. Table 1.1 shows a numerical example of this income-mul-
tiplication process.

In Table 1.1, imagine that something caused the interest rate to
fall, and this stimulated an increase in investment spending of Mu. 100.
Round after round the money was spent and respent, with 40 percent
leaking out of the income-generating stream each time. Finally, when
nothing was left to be respent, the original Mu. 100 increase had generated a cumulative increase 2.5 times larger. In this case, the multiplier would be calculated as 2.5; that is, every initial increase of
Mu. 1 will multiply to a total increase of Mu. 2.5. The multiplier is
arithmetically determined as 1 divided by the leakage fraction. In
Table 1.1, the leakage fraction was 40 percent, and $1 \div .40 = 2.5$.

This means that the more spending leaks out into taxes, imports, savings, and the like, the smaller will be the multiplier and the income generated.

In both the economics of nations and the economics of regions, the essential factors in analyzing growth or decline in income are the same: the levels of the four components of spending on the one hand, and the multiplier, as determined by the magnitudes of the leakages, on the other.

When we examine the factors that determine levels of spending and the factors that determine the value of the multiplier, however, we find significant differences between the economies of nations and the economies of regions or local areas. In most countries, domestic consumption is determined largely by how much people have to spend and how willing they are to spend it; in most regions an additional factor of major consequence is the willingness to spend in the region and on products made in the region. In most countries, private domestic investment is determined largely by the availability of investment capital and the attractiveness of investing it; in most regions an additional factor of major consequence is the availability of capital and relative attractiveness of investment opportunities in the particular subnational area. Government spending nationally is determined by authorities internal to the system; government spending in a region may be determined largely by authorities outside the region. Exports from the country can be encouraged and imports to the country can be discouraged through a variety of devices available to the national government; municipal, provincial, or regional governments generally do not have such devices available to them. Furthermore, many of the leakages from the income-generating stream, such as taxes and savings, are not actually "lost" to the national economy. Taxes or savings that leak out this year may return as government spending or investment next year. That is far less likely to be the case in a region.

Indeed, the conventional national-income-determination model tends to view the economy as a more or less closed environment that exists at a point in space. Income is determined largely by what goes on within the system; and the interest rate, government spending, investment, saving, the multiplier, and so on happen in a spaceless place. It is clear that, by contrast, income in a particular region may be determined no less, and perhaps more, by what goes on outside the regional borders than by what goes on within them. A high rate of interest nationally may be reflected in a flight of capital from the region. A relatively high national multiplier may arise from factors that cause the multiplier of a particular region to be low. The region or local area faces political and resource-allocation

problems quite different from those of the nation, because it com-
petes with other places spread throughout the national territory. The
region can lose income and resources to the rest of the world or gain
income and resources from the rest of the world to a relative degree
generally unknown to countries.

SOME IMPLICATIONS FOR REGIONAL-
DEVELOPMENT PLANNING

This understanding of the differences between national and regional economies draws our attention to three major implications for
regional-development planning practitioners. The first is that for
development planning purposes, regional economic analysis requires
a thorough examination of the region and of the national environment
of which it is part, a determination of the natures of the links through
which the two interact, and an evaluation of the ultimate impacts
these interactions have upon the region.

The second is that what appears to be good for the nation may
not necessarily be good for each of its regions, and what is good for
a region may not necessarily be good for the nation. As an illustration, let us suppose that a plant for the processing of agricultural
produce were established in a rural region that had formerly sent
its produce to a distant city, its principal market, for processing.
The new plant might provide employment for regional surplus farm
labor and increase the regional multiplier by eliminating the need to
"import" from the distant city the processed product produced in the
plant. It might thereby have an extremely beneficial effect on the
level of regional income. However, transfer of the processing to the
hinterland may result in the displacement of higher-paid urban workers and, through a negative multiplier effect, ultimately reduce the
GNP. Moreover, the displaced urban workers who have thus been
removed from the tax base may now constitute, together with their
families, a greater drain on the national public-services budget.

Or, take the example of a national urbanization trend that may
be looked upon favorably by government authorities. To their minds,
it may reflect a relocation of surplus rural labor that facilitates a
national industrialization program without inflation. The hinterland
region, however, may be losing people from the villages and small
towns who perform important services for the farming population;
and the farms may be losing those who are the ablest, most productive, and most innovative.

This is not to say that the region must be viewed as necessarily
at odds with the nation. Indeed, proper regional-development planning
involves the integration of regional- and national-development objec-

tives for the maximum benefit of both, one of the major regional-development planning challenges.

The third implication for regional-development planning is that institutional tools available for regional development—the administrative and policy-making bodies and authorities—are quite different at the regional level from those available at the national level; and even if this were not the case, the same policy alternatives would not be available at both levels. For example, at the national level a reallocation of resources for development can be brought about by printing money and using it for development investment. This causes inflation and a reduction of the demands on resources to satisfy requirements of consumer-goods production. It is easy to see that, for better or for worse, such a policy could not be pursued at the regional level. And if it could be attempted, it would no doubt be relatively ineffective because of diffusion across the region's open borders.

INTRAREGIONAL LINKAGES

Just as the region must be understood as a piece of the national economic fabric, so also it should be understood as composed of interconnected subregional places. Interactions among these places can be of a nature that contributes to or detracts from regional welfare and development. In examining the region and helping to plan, the analyst must attempt to identify and account for important intraregional linkages that do or could influence the efficiency and equity of development.

Suppose that to create employment in a poor region the national government located a bicycle assembly factory there, or provided incentives for a private investor to do so. For purposes of efficiency, the factory is sited in the largest town in the region, which also appears to be where the unemployed people are concentrated. All the bicycle parts are "imported" from elsewhere in the country, and all the profits are "exported" to the central government or the private investor. So of all the spending by the factory, only a portion, say 40 percent, is spent in the region, mainly on wages of factory workers; the rest, 60 percent, leaks out.

Now imagine that in addition to this town there are several smaller towns, each a market town for an agricultural subarea of the region. And instead of a bicycle factory, regional-development planners, aware of potential intraregional multiplier effects, persuaded the government to invest in a cold-storage plant. Only 15 percent of the plant's expenditures goes for wages; another 75 percent pays for farm produce to be stored; another 10 percent is profits exported out of the region. Although the cold-storage plant employs fewer people than the bicycle factory, the 75 percent of expenditures paid for farm produce is spent among the smaller market towns, most of it ultimately going to farmers in the region. The farmers tend to spend much more of their income locally than do workers in the main regional town, which includes spending it on goods and services purchased directly or indirectly from the main regional town. The cold-storage capability expands the effective market for regional farm produce, so farm incomes in the region increase. Moreover, people who live in the region can substitute purchases from the cold-storage facility for products that were previously imported to the region.

Investment in the cold-storage facility may at first appear of lesser benefit to the town in which it is located, since from the perspective of that town it employs fewer people and has expenditure leakages of 85 percent. But from the regional perspective, the leakage is only 10 percent, and the increased incomes and higher regional spending multipliers of the farmers, together with the increased multiplier resulting from import substitution, ultimately mean higher incomes throughout the region. In the end, more employment may even be created in the major town through intraregional multiplier effects.

There are other aspects of intraregional linkages that must be considered. What is the dynamic of rural-urban economic relationships within the region? What is the pattern of urban-urban interactions? Is there a hierarchy of urban places, or some other pattern of settlement with an efficiently distributed network of services and functions? Are there different types of networks for different types of functions? How are, or can, the appropriate balances be achieved between the benefits of scale and the benefits of dispersion?

Many of the methods of analysis presented in the following chapters can be used to explore actual and potential relationships within the regional space. Methods of interregional analysis can be used for intraregional analysis as well. If a multiplier or location quotient can be computed for a region, it can also be computed for subregional towns or areas and represented graphically on a map. Methods of analysis that compare the region with the country can also be used to compare the urban or rural subspace of the region, or a major town or a central city area, with the rest of the region. It is assumed hereafter that the reader or user of this book is aware that the regional economy is not only relatively open but also has an internal dynamic that is at the heart of its regional functioning. And it is anticipated, therefore, that the methods presented will be creatively modified and expanded to serve the spatial-analysis needs of the region or local area in question.

THREE MODELS OF LONG-TERM
REGIONAL DEVELOPMENT

What happens to the work of the regional analyst? It is used
as part of a regional-development planning process to guide decisions
about near-term actions and investments to be undertaken in order
to promote permanent improvement in the economic welfare of the
region's residents. Some discussion about the general planning process, on the one hand, and individual project considerations, on the
other, will be found in Part III of this book.

Both in analyzing the past and present through descriptive
methods of regional analysis and in making recommendations and decisions that will help shape the future, it is useful to have in mind
some general frames of reference. Methods of analysis do not produce analysis, only numbers. The analyst interprets these numbers
so that they tell a story that provides guidance for planning. In the
following paragraphs, three models of long-term regional development are suggested as general frames of reference for analysis and
planning. They are, of course, notional models only. None will be
found in reality as it is presented here; yet, they do encompass the
dominant themes running through the literature and practice of regional development today. They are meant to create images in the
minds of analysts and planners that will help them turn economic
analysis into development analysis. In what ways, it might be asked,
does the economic analysis of the region suggest a likeness to one
of the models? In what ways is the region in question different from
each of the models? Does it combine elements of different models?
Which model, or what combination of them, provides the best framework for equitable and efficient development consistent with regional
values and national goals?

Figure 1.1 provides an impressionistic overview of the three
basic models of long-term regional development. The characteristics
associated with each model are summarized in Table 1.2.

In the growth pole model, the region is thought of as comprising
a major town with a loosely defined hinterland. Because the major
town, the growth pole, already has a concentration of population and
economic activity, it features the best linkages to a metropolitan
center outside the region, economies of scale, and economies of agglomeration (economies arising from the location of different kinds
of economic activity near each other) in the region. This gives the
growth pole the foundation for a self-reinforcing growth dynamic
and makes it the most economically efficient location for significant
nonfarm investments. Development is based mainly on production
for the exchange economy (that is, production for trade outside the
region). When an enterprise in the growth pole thrives, benefits

FIGURE 1.1

Three Models of Long-term Regional Development

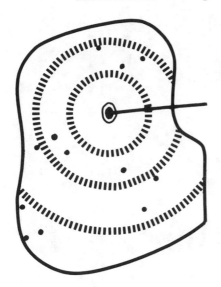

Growth Pole
- Emphasis on exchange economy.
- Development benefits through ripple effects from concentrated investments.
- Principally export-based linkage from the regional growth pole to the primate city.

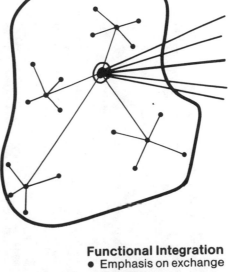

Functional Integration
- Emphasis on exchange economy.
- Development benefits through intraregional linkages fostered by dispersed investments.
- Diverse functional linkages to other regions.

Decentralized Territorial Integration
- Emphasis on use economy.
- Development benefits through subregional self-sufficiency fostered by locally determined dispersed investments.
- Selective closure.

11

TABLE 1.2

Summary Characteristics of the Models of Long-term Regional Development

Characteristic	Growth Pole	Functional Integration	Decentralized Territorial Integration
Emphasis on exchange or use economy?	Emphasis on exchange economy	Emphasis on exchange economy, but attention to use economy also	Emphasis on use economy
How are development benefits distributed?	Through ripple effects from concentrated investments in the growth pole, the main regional town	Through intraregional linkages fostered by investments strategically dispersed throughout the region	Through subregional self-sufficiency fostered by locally determined dispersed investments
What is the dynamic of intraregional linkages?	Economies of agglomeration in the growth pole, which supplies production, commercial, and administrative services for the region. Spontaneous market links to the rest of the region	Linkages form a "rational system" based on economically optimal locations of functions within the region, and are highly coordinated	Selective linkages. Economic production, distribution, and planning linkages evolve organically over time
What is the nature of interregional linkages?	Concentrated on exports from the growth pole to a metropolitan center outside the region, and imports of supplies and consumer goods to the growth pole	Diversified linkages to other regions, primarily but not only through the main regional town	Selective closure to minimize dependency and vulnerability of the region to external economic forces. Selected linkages with other regions fostered
How is intraregional coordination accomplished?	Mainly through spontaneous market mechanisms	Mainly through a framework of institutionalized planning and coordination mechanisms that work largely on a top-down basis	Mainly through selective bottom-up mechanisms that evolve organically over time
What is the economic growth orientation?	Maximize undifferentiated economic growth	Long-term growth optimization. Explicit concern with distributional aspects of growth	Economic growth, as such, secondary to self-sufficiency and self-determination
What is the nature of the associated development planning process, if any?	Centralized planning based on economic cost-benefit considerations of individual projects	Integrated centralized/decentralized planning; "disaggregative," highly technical, interdisciplinary	Decentralized planning; "aggregative," merges technical and popular input
What is the associated view of national space?	The nation is made up of regional modules connected to metropolitan centers	The nation is a structured hierarchy of central places and their hinterlands	The nation is a loosely structured federation of regions, each a loose cluster of subregional areas

ripple like waves throughout the region owing to market mechanisms that link the growth pole to its hinterland. A new factory in the growth pole, for example, may purchase supplies and services directly or indirectly from the hinterland and generate increased income that also directly and indirectly expands the effective markets of farmers, workers, businesses, and tradespeople in the surrounding area; all these will expand their production in response.

The growth pole model is based on the view that the prosperity of the region derives from the profitability and growth of its economic enterprises, and that the nonagricultural enterprises upon which sustained growth depends will be most profitable if located in the growth pole. Economic growth is seen as roughly synonymous with economic development and, therefore, should be maximized. The only economic development planning that is needed is for infrastructure that will support a favorable economic environment in the growth pole and for enterprises that will prosper and grow there. The nation is seen as comprised of regional modules, each effectively represented by a growth pole linked to a national metropolitan center.

In the functional integration model, the region is thought of as a relatively organized network of places with, for example, farms clustered about villages, villages clustered about market towns, market towns clustered about subregional towns, and subregional towns clustered about the regional town. Each scale and type of economic function has its optimum location in the region and in the hierarchy based upon regional efficiency considerations. Places and subareas in the region are relatively specialized, and regional efficiency means integrating their absolute and comparative advantages in a way that maximizes overall regional prosperity. Development is based mainly on production for the exchange economy, but development benefits are seen explicitly as being distributed through linkages to production for the use economy (that is, production to serve regional needs directly). Investments in farms, infrastructure, and enterprises are carefully calculated to be dispersed throughout the region in a manner that exploits, creates, and reinforces the efficiencies of intraregional linkages.

The functional integration model is based on the view that since population and economic activity of necessity are distributed in space, a deliberate effort is warranted to make that space work for the benefit of the region; and further, that sustained growth requires development to be distributed over regional space through the functional integration of its villages and towns. This may require different investment priorities in different locations from those that would prevail with only the profitability of specific enterprises in mind. Extensive and relatively formal planning and coordinating mechanisms are needed, and they can usually only be provided through centralized institutional frameworks. However, the nature of planning and co-ordinating functional integration over the space of a region is such that the centralized planning framework tends to incorporate planning functions carried out at lower levels. Planning tends to be disaggregative—that is, national development goals are disaggregated to the regional level, where they are in turn disaggregated to subregional areas. The nation is seen as a structured hierarchy of central places and their hinterlands, a system of regions, each region having a variety of functional linkages to other regions.

In the decentralized territorial integration model the region is thought of as a loosely connected collection of subareas, each with a more or less articulated structure of settlements. Emphasis is on the use economy of each subarea and the region, with development being measured more in terms of relative self-sufficiency than in terms of volume of production for trade. The region and its subareas are encouraged first in small-scale production for local markets, with only selective linkages through the regional and national settlement hierarchy. Development investment is determined by, or at least with participation of, people from the towns and villages of the region. Regional planning therefore is decentralized, merges popular and technical input, and is aggregative—that is, regional goals are derived by aggregating subregional goals.

The decentralized territorial integration model is based on the view that regions and their subareas should have the capacity to plan and implement development activity with their own self-sufficiency in mind. This means that investments to develop planning and management capacity at subregional and regional levels should parallel investments in economic projects at those levels. This perception of regional development holds further that over time stable and prospering subregional economies discover advantages to linking with other places in the region for selected functions, so that gradually and organically regional networks of services, of enterprises, and of planning and coordinating mechanisms do emerge to various degrees. Regional economic integration is said to come about with increasing economic mass, maturity, modernity, and mutuality of interest (the "four M's") among the places and local areas within the region. From an economic perspective, the nation is seen as a loosely structured federation of regions.

These three models of long-term regional economic development can be modified and adapted to national economic contexts that rely heavily on free-market mechanisms as well as to those that rely more on central planning. In the first case, the key regional planning question may be how to acquire and use resources for market responses that will foster long-term economic development. In the latter case, the key regional planning question may be how to use

TABLE 1.3

Summary of the Descriptive Methods of Regional Analysis

Method (follows the order of presentation in Part II of this book)	Dominant Analytical Question	Dominant Analytical View of the Region		
		Unit in Relation to the Country	Unit Interacting with the Country	Interacting Subregional Areas
Basic regional statistical compendium	What is the overall regional economic profile?	X		
Income measures	What are the levels of different types of income in the region?	X		
Income and product accounts	What is the value of regional economic production and how is this reflected in different types of income in the region?	X		
Linkage studies	What are the forward/backward linkages across regional borders or within subregional areas?		X	X
Gravity studies	What is the intensity of actual and potential interaction among selected places?		X	X
Flow studies	How much of what commodities flows from selected points of origin to selected points of destination?		X	X
Balance-of-payments statements	What is the value of flows across the region's borders?		X	
Mix-and-share analysis	What is the relative industrial composition of the region and how is it changing?	X		
Location quotient and related measures	What is the degree of relative specialization of the region in selected industries?	X		
Economic-base analysis	What is the relationship between exogenous demand for the region's products and regional economic expansion?		X	
Regional input-output analysis	What are the regional interindustry linkages in terms of inputs and outputs, as related to exogenous demand?		X	

available resources to respond to central government production targets in a manner that best fosters long-term regional development.
In either case, the models are likely to be useful as reference points
for developing a unique schema to describe the long-term development of the region in the past or for formulating one to guide the long-
term development of the region in the future.

THE DESCRIPTIVE METHODS

A good way to begin the economic analysis of a particular region
or local area is to write a broad description of it in terms of its openness, spatial relations, and overall pattern of development as reflected
in its principal economic activities, its structure, and the lives of
the people who live there. This description should be based on experience and readily available information rather than on extensive
statistical research. It will serve as a good starting frame of reference that can help in determining which methods of analysis are
most urgently needed and how they should be reshaped to serve the
situation at hand.

The descriptive methods of regional analysis discussed in the
chapters of Part II provide different angles of insight into the way a
region works. The specific perspectives of different types of methods
are suggested by the titles of the chapters in which they appear. They
can, however, also be grouped into three broader categories based
on their overall analytical views of the region. There are those that
view the region as a unit in relation to other regions and the country;
there are those that view the region as a unit interacting with other
regions and the country; and there are those that view the region as
composed of interacting subregional areas. As suggested earlier,
with some slight but imaginative modification, methods generally
thought of as representing one view can often be made to serve
another analytical view as well. A summary of the methods is presented in Table 1.3.

Though descriptive methods of analysis can often be used as
part of an exercise meant to simulate and predict the future, they
are presented here because of their value as devices for explaining
and understanding a region's past and present. They provide a means
of observing and evaluating the way in which land, labor, and capital
have interacted over the space of a region and in relation to the region's relative location within a larger system. They do not provide
solutions to planning problems. They provide, rather, support and
guidance for the regional or local development-planning process by
serving as tools that help to disclose the real nature and dynamics
of the regional economy.

PART II

METHODS OF
REGIONAL
ECONOMIC ANALYSIS

2

THE BASIC REGIONAL
STATISTICAL
COMPENDIUM

Data collection is often one of the first and major tasks of a
regional-development planning staff. It is a task that can be costly
in terms of time, labor, and development funds. If the collection is
not performed systematically, it will later be found that some data
obtained are useless and that some that are needed have not been obtained. And, in the end, available data may determine the nature of
the analyses performed, instead of the other way around. It is desirable, then, prior to the collection of detailed data, to work out a
preliminary analysis framework. This framework may be made up
of several analysis methods, such as those found in the following chapters, each designed to provide the basis for a deeper understanding
of a particular aspect of the regional complex. The chapters of Part
III have more to say about designing a preliminary framework.

Even before a framework of analysis can be contemplated seriously, however, some preparatory work must be done to provide the
development team with a broad familiarity with the region or local area
and with a basis for determining the types of analysis tools needed
and feasible. This preparatory work can take the form of the sort of
broad description mentioned in the previous chapter; but it can then
go beyond that to a basic regional statistical compendium. "Statistical compendium" refers to a document made up of statistical tables,
usually accompanied by diagrams, charts, maps, and explanatory
text, covering a wide range of subjects important to a preliminary
understanding of a region's unique nature.

FUNCTIONS OF THE COMPENDIUM

A regional profile in the form of a statistical compendium has
the potential to fulfill a great many functions. It can serve to help

present the region's case to agencies of the central government and other potential sources of development resources, and it provides concrete evidence that development work is in progress. For the local leadership, whose support is essential for the development effort, the compendium provides an introduction to the broad array of regional problems and potentials.

For the development staff, the completed compendium will not only provide the basis for selecting areas for further intensive study, but it will also facilitate a preliminary overall analysis of the region and the establishment of initial planning and implementation priorities.

The task of designing and putting together the compendium often constitutes the first effort that has a tangible and immediate objective and that requires the coordinated participation of the entire development team. As such, the effort helps crystallize working relationships and areas of specialization among development workers. Beyond this, work on the compendium provides a framework for a first systematic review of the entire regional complex by the development team, brings about contacts with concerned bodies in the region, and familiarizes the analysts with sources, types, and characteristics of regional data available and unavailable for future reference.

It is probably unnecessary to dwell on the importance of data in the development planning process for regions and local areas. If anything, the collection and processing of statistical data too often are seen as the essence of planning, as if planning were a problem the correct solution to which could be obtained by following the appropriate mechanical procedures. Sight should not be lost of the fact that the planning process is an attempt at reasoned decision making based on human values, experience, and judgments, supported by statistical information processed and presented in useful form. Chapter 11, "The General Planning Process: From Goals to Projects," contains a brief discussion of the role of data in general in the planning process. For the present it is sufficient to stress that compilation of the basic regional statistical compendium is an effort worth undertaking only with great care to ensure that it assists in advancing both the planning process and its supporting analyses.

COMPONENTS OF COMPENDIUM TABLES

Usually, the maps, charts, diagrams, and text of a regional compendium are based on the statistical tables that make up the heart of the document. When considering how the set of tables might be designed, there are four basic structural components concerning which decisions must be made. These components are as follows (see Figure 2.1):

FIGURE 2.1

Illustration of a Compendium Table and Its Components

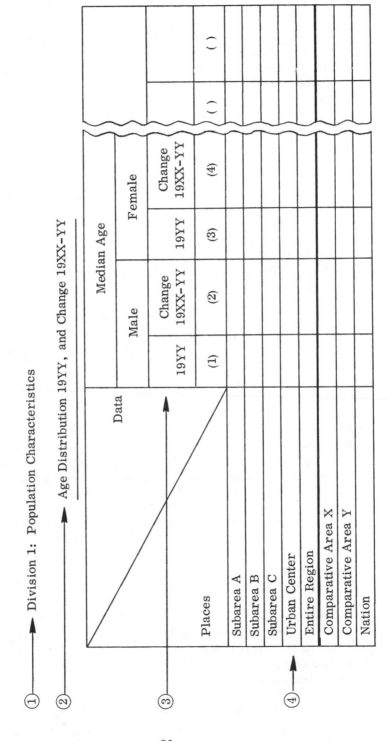

① → Division 1: Population Characteristics

② → Age Distribution 19YY, and Change 19XX-YY

③ →

④ →

Data / Places	Median Age					
	Male		Female			
	19YY	Change 19XX-YY	19YY	Change 19XX-YY		
	(1)	(2)	(3)	(4)	( )	( )
Subarea A						
Subarea B						
Subarea C						
Urban Center						
Entire Region						
Comparative Area X						
Comparative Area Y						
Nation						

1. <u>Overall analytical rubrics</u>: the compendium divisions, or broad subject categories;
2. <u>Table titles</u>: the specific subjects dealt with by the tables within each division;
3. <u>Column headings</u>: the specific data selected to describe the subject with which each table is concerned;
4. <u>Row headings</u>: comprising the list of geographic areas for which the data indicated in each column heading are provided.

Tables do not have to follow the format of the illustration in Figure 2.1, but whatever the format design, the components remain essentially the same. Decisions made regarding them will determine the quality and quantity of information about the region that will be communicated by the statistical data in the compendium.

CONSIDERATIONS IN THE CHOICE OF OVERALL ANALYTICAL RUBRICS AND TABLE SUBJECTS

The overall analytical rubrics, broad subject categories or divisions of the compendium into which the statistical tables are organized, should not be a matter of arbitrary convenience. They cause data to be presented in a manner that promotes viewing the region in accordance with a certain analytical orientation. Chapter 11 points out that the set of analytical rubrics can be used as an organizing framework throughout the planning process, promoting clarity and consistency as the process progresses from one step to the next. Thus, while these categories of information can and probably will be revised as the planning process matures, their initial selection is sufficiently basic to the planning frame of reference to warrant a good deal of careful thought. The only fixed rule is that taken together they must in some sense reflect the relevant whole.

For example, one government agency in the United States charged with a particular concern for the welfare of the poor in its development activities published guidelines for local statistical compendiums that called for major compendium divisions in accordance with the following analytical rubrics:

Profile of the poor
General demographic characteristics
Geographic characteristics
Economic characteristics
Social characteristics

At the same time, another U.S. government agency charged with a particular focus on unemployment and community development used the following set of analytical rubrics to organize the statistical compendiums for areas it assisted:

Characteristics of the unemployed
Community facilities
General population characteristics
Economic structure and activities
Physical resources

In each of these cases the tables of the statistical compendium obviously were organized in a manner meant to reflect the specific legislated mission of the particular agency.

One approach often used is the regional resources or assets approach, in which all the features of the region are seen as greater or lesser resources that can be utilized to advance economic development. The set of specific analytical rubrics devised would reflect the dominant exploitable features of the particular area. In an area dependent upon extractive industry, the analytical rubrics might be

Human resources
Institutional resources
Energy resources
Mineral resources
Timber resources

Imagination can be used to consider how the analytical rubrics might appear under this approach in an area heavily dependent upon tourism, or manufacturing, or agriculture, or upon a combination.

Another approach often used is known as the HINCO view of the region or local area. Tables are organized under analytical rubrics highlighting the human, institutional, natural, capital, and other components of the regional complex. This approach has been found especially useful as a working framework for a community participatory planning process that builds upon work on the basic regional statistical compendium. Table 2.1 illustrates the subjects of tables that might appear in each division of a compendium organized along HINCO lines.

Many regional and local economic planners prefer sets of analytical rubrics that cause the compendium to highlight aspects of the area that relate more directly to key economic planning issues as they perceive them. Thus, they have often promoted organizing compendium tables into categories such as social aspects, physical aspects, institutional aspects, and economic aspects, with this latter category further subdivided into regional export-related activities, regional

TABLE 2.1

Illustrative Compendium Model Organized according to the HINCO Approach

Analytical Rubric	Table Subjects
1. Human aspects	Population size and demographic characteristics
	Education
	Work experience, skills
	Income and wages
	Expenditure patterns
	Employment, unemployment, labor force participation
	Health
	Population subsets (for example, minorities, rural, urban)
	Housing
	Productivity
	Commutation
	Labor-market areas
2. Institutional aspects	Regional and local governments
	Public revenue and expenditure patterns
	Social and municipal services
	Labor-to-capital ratios
	Business barriers
	Business institutions
	Institutional coordination
	Institutional participation
	Trade and labor organizations
	Cooperatives
	Economic activity mix characteristics
	Landownership patterns
3. Natural aspects	Land-use patterns
	Mineral resources

24

Soil types
Water resources
Topographic features
Recreation assets
Scenic assets
Locational characteristics
Historic sites
Other heritage—related features
Environmentally sensitive zones
Hazard—prone zones

4. Capital aspects

Infrastructure
Land—use potentials
Transportation and communication
Public investment
Private investment
Savings rates
External capital sources
Housing stock
Unutilized/underutilized structures
Firm size
Concentration ratios
Gross product
Capital-to-output ratios
Public—capital construction

5. Other aspects

Development plans and planning at higher and lower levels
Trade areas
Special relationships with other areas
Special information on major economic activities, problems, or potentials
Results of surveys designed to obtain the views of the leadership or the general public on development problems, potentials, or desired directions
Energy resources

25

TABLE 2.2

Illustrative Compendium Model Organized according to the Population–Location–Activities Approach

Analytical Rubric	Table Subjects	Insights Provided
1. Population and social characteristics	Population size, age distribution, family characteristics, vital statistics, growth components, and so on Education Work experience Income and wealth Personal income and expenditure patterns (sources and uses) Employment and unemployment, labor–force participation, worker–to–total–population ratio, and so on Health, living conditions, and so on Welfare Government Subsets, for example, farmers, minorities, rural population, urban population, and so on	Status, problems, and potentials of human resources; social organization; local culture, and so on
2. Location characteristics	Physical resources Other natural geographic, locational, climatic features, and so on Social capital, infrastructure, and rates and sources of investment in these Governments Inter– and intraregional orientations and spatial relationships Transportation and communication mixes and links	Spatial and physical qualities of the location, both natural and man–made, including general inter– and intraregional lines of communication, commerce, and central–place hierarchy patterns
3. Economic activities	Firm size Concentration ratios	Levels and types of economic activities, industrial linkages, producer or con–

26

characteristics	Value added Gross regional product Productivity Sales Farm characteristics Detailed characteristics of major economic activities Investments and capital accumulation Capital-to-output ratios Industry-mix characteristics	sumer goods orientations, local and export consumption orientations, investment, credit, and other aspects of the region's structure of economic activities
4. Population-location-relationships characteristics	Population extent, density, and frequency measures, for example, population per square mile, location and extent of population centers, distribution of settlements by population size, distribution of population by settlements and settlement size, and so on Travel patterns Commutation External travel Migration Landownership patterns	The manner in which the characteristics of the population and of the location result in and result from interactions between them
5. Population-activity-relationships characteristics	Employment by industry Income and wages by industry Unemployment by industry experience Labor-to-capital ratios Labor productivity by industry	How efficiently human resources are being utilized in economic activity, and the benefit to the population from engaging in the activities and utilizing the technologies prevailing in the region
6. Location-activity-relationships characteristics	Location of commerce and industry Intra- and interregional flows and linkages Trade areas Labor market areas Special relationships with other regions	The characteristics, problems, and potentials of economic activity as related to and determined by spatial and physical features of the regional location

import-related activities, and regional activities that serve regional markets. A variation on this approach involves subdividing economic aspects into extractive, manufacturing, commerce, agricultural, and perhaps tourism subcomponents.

Table 2.2 is an illustration of a compendium model based on a population-location-activities approach, specifically oriented to high-lighting not only what goes on within a region, but also how this is related to the region's location. The locational characteristics have both a physical dimension and a relative spatial dimension. Table 2.2 suggests the analytical rubrics and the table subjects that could be included under each rubric. It also provides a brief summary of the contributions that data within each division of the compendium might make toward a comprehensive regional description.

Neither Table 2.1 nor Table 2.2 are suggested as checklists of requirements for basic regional statistical compendiums. First efforts to design such compendiums should certainly aim at less ambitious un-dertakings than the illustrations might imply. As planning efforts continue over the years, there will be time enough to modify, elab-orate, and expand the compendium. It is rather important, especially when preparation of the compendium is used as a means of launching a planning effort, not to be trapped by the idea that the compendium must in some sense be absolutely complete before further analysis and planning work can continue. Tables 2.1 and 2.2 should be used only as broad guides, from which selections can be made as appropri-ate to the circumstances and data availabilities that prevail.

The purpose of the set of overall analytical rubrics that dictate the organization of the compendium is to isolate the major components of the regional or local socioeconomic system in order better to ob-serve and understand the functioning of the whole. But it is important to remember that the whole really is a system and that the links and in-terdependencies among the various components must not be overlooked. A relaxed attitude should be taken concerning subjects that do not fall neatly under one rubric or another. Matters that common sense sug-gests ought to be viewed as a unit should not be chopped up in order to fit within the strict definitional bounds of separate analytical rubrics. There will undoubtedly be overlap among subjects handled under the various analytical rubrics, and this may lead here and there to the repetition of data presented. Overlap and repetition will be noticed, for example, in both Tables 2.1 and 2.2. That is to be expected when dealing with so complex a system as a regional or local economy.

CONSIDERATIONS IN THE DESIGN OF COLUMN HEADINGS

The design of the column headings of a table reflects the selec-tion of measures and indicators thought most appropriate for describ-

ing the subject with which the table deals from among those for which
data are available. Column headings may call for absolute measures,
such as regional income, and they may call as well for processed
data computed from absolute measures, such as percentage increases
in regional income. Processed data usually involve a comparison of
absolute measures over time or over space, or both.

Intertemporal comparisons or interareal comparisons are usually accomplished by means of percentage changes or indexes, both
of which are merely ratio computations. Ratio computations are the
simplest of all methods of analysis—that is, the simplest of all devices for processing absolute measures; and as many of the following
chapters will show, they are usually the point of departure for the
more elaborate methods, such as input-output analysis.

Table 2.3 shows unemployment for a province and for the nation in 19XX and 19YY, say the beginning and end of a five-year period, in the leftmost columns. A first ratio computation converts
these numbers into unemployment rates (figures for the total labor
force are not shown), which increases the available information by
revealing the proportion not able to find work from among those able
and willing to work. The unemployment rates are shown in columns
3 and 4. On casual observation, the figures in columns 3 and 4 indicate that while the rate of unemployment in the province showed improvement over the period 19XX-19YY, it compared rather unfavorably with the nation in both years. How unfavorably? And was the
position of the province improving or deteriorating in relation to the
nation over the period?

A further ratio calculation, a ratio of ratios, shows in column
5 that the decrease in unemployment in the province lagged behind
that of the country. Thus, while columns 3 and 4 show that the provincial unemployment rate declined by 1.0 compared with 1.7 for the
nation, column 5 shows that, in fact, the decline in the provincial rate
amounted to only 12.8 percent, compared with a decline of 15.6 percent for the nation. The intertemporal ratio computation has thereby
further increased the available information from the absolute measures.

Columns 6 and 7 of Table 2.3 carry the analysis a step further
and provide a quantification of what intuition has probably already
suggested. If the decline in unemployment in the province has been
slower than in the nation as a whole, then despite the improvement in
the provincial unemployment rate, its position relative to the nation
must have deteriorated over the period. Interareal indexes using national unemployment rates as the base were computed from columns
3 and 4. As a matter of convention, the ratios were multiplied by 100
to convert them to whole numbers, with 100 representing the base
for comparison. Columns 6 and 7 show higher unemployment in the

TABLE 2.3

Illustration of Intertemporal and Interareal Comparisons

	Number of Unemployed People		Unemployment Rates				
			19XX	19YY	Percentage Change,	National Indexes,	
	19XX	19YY			19XX-19YY	19XX	19YY
	(1)	(2)	(3)	(4)	(5)	(6)	(7)
Province	6,000	5,440	7.8	6.8	-12.8	173	179
Nation	850,000	760,000	4.5	3.8	-15.6	100	100

region relative to the nation at the end of the period than at the beginning of the period. This suggests a growing polarization between the province and other areas that could have extremely serious consequences for the province over the long run, especially if something were to cause the general decline in unemployment to be arrested.

Obviously, this business of ratio computations can be taken to extremes. One could compute a ratio of percentage changes shown in column 5, a ratio of national indexes shown in columns 6 and 7, and so on. Clearly, good judgment has to be exercised in designing column headings both in terms of selecting absolute measures and in terms of the ratio computations called for.

CONSIDERATIONS IN THE DESIGN
OF ROW HEADINGS

The geographic areas listed in the row headings (often referred to as the table stub) may include the region's principal towns and subareas and also the reference areas outside the region selected as norms for comparison. The reference areas provide a background against which to consider local data.

National figures are popular as standards of comparison, and this is reasonable because national figures reflect the larger environment of which the region is a part. But for many regions, particularly rural ones, national socioeconomic measures are often of questionable comparative value. In the first place, a major component in the calculation of national figures may be an urbanized population whose tastes, needs, standards, and way of life in general are very different from those prevailing in the nonurbanized areas. Second, a comparison with the national average, median, or the like, while in a sense a comparison with a national composite, is not a comparison with anything that exists. People concerned with economic development at the local level most frequently view their region and its progress relative to other specific regions or local areas. In many cases, then, other reference areas are needed as standards of comparison in addition to or instead of the nation.

There is a wide variety of alternatives to the national norm as standards of comparison. Other possible reference areas include other regions, medians or averages of all other regions, medians or averages of selected groups of other regions, and so on. In the search for a standard of comparison to complement or replace the nation in the row headings of a particular table, the analyst may look for real or fictitious (composite) areas that are similar to the region under study in terms of population size or social, economic, and cultural characteristics, or that have a functional similarity. The standard of comparison that would be most meaningful would depend on the subject with which the table deals and the point to be made.

CONCLUDING REMARKS

Some factors critical to an understanding of a region and its past and potential development may not lend themselves to quantification or to presentation in a tabular format, even of the simple type discussed in this chapter. This may be especially true in regions where, for example, factors such as social mobility and stratification may be decisive in development efforts but may resist meaningful expression in statistical form; or the data may be unobtainable. This may be true as well with regard to certain aspects of the quality of the human or natural environment in the region or local area. In such cases it may be advisable to arrange for a special supplement to the statistical compendium to deal with nonquantifiable social, cultural, institutional, environmental, or other elements of the regional complex.

EXERCISES FOR CHAPTER 2

   1. Describe an appropriate compendium model for your region
or local area. Explain why it is particularly suited. Design one sample table under each analytical rubric.
   2. Consider Table 2.3 and the discussion surrounding it. Work
up a numerical example based on data from your own region and country that demonstrates the same point (your example need not deal
with unemployment).
   3. Suppose your country is composed of five regions. One is
urban, contains 25 percent of the total population, and has an annual
average family money income about four times that prevailing in the
rural regions. The other four regions are agricultural and are of
about equal size in population. No precise determination of the size
of in-kind incomes of rural families has been made, but they are
known to be significant. If you are working with a rural region, what
might be an appropriate norm for comparison?

   The nation (national averages)?
   The rural subspace (rural averages)?
   The median region (median regional values)?
   The median rural region (median rural regional values)?
   Some other, or a combination?

Explain your choice, and explain why certain norms might be appropriate for some subjects that are being investigated but not for others.
Give examples.
   4. The second analytical rubric of Table 2.2, "Location characteristics," includes the subject "Inter- and intraregional orienta-
tions and spatial relationships." One useful table/map dealing with
this subject might be "Regional Market Centers," showing major market centers and indicating their trade areas. It would make sense to
include market centers outside the region with trade areas that extend
into the region. What restrictions should be placed on the scope of
such a table/map so that the information is manageable but useful?
What column and row headings might appear in the table?

3

INCOME MEASURES,
INCOME-AND-PRODUCT
ACCOUNTS

Regional income measures are important because they provide indications of personal and community welfare and, compared over time, of economic growth. Regional income-and-product accounts can be designed to provide the same thing and more. They can be a powerful tool for description and analysis of a region's economic structure, and can be made to reflect an underlying social, geographic, sectoral, or other substructure as well. The greatest danger in using these methods of regional analysis is, perhaps, in the tendency to overstress their significance as against other methods of analysis.

GENERAL CAVEATS

A change in (real) regional income is usually taken to imply a change in welfare in the same direction. But a number of important issues arise when using measures of income as indicators of welfare. Does an increase in income always mean an increase in welfare for the community? For the entire community? And does the absence of an increase in income always imply that progress in economic development has not taken place? How can meaningful recognition be made of nonmonetary (in-kind) income? What is the relationship between income, a flow concept, and wealth, a stock concept, as regards regional welfare and development?

Gross regional product (GRP) is commonly viewed as a good comprehensive indicator of regional economic health and long-term development. As such, it suffers the same shortcomings as the traditional gross national product (GNP) when used similarly at the national level. First is the fact that it measures only economic product —that is, products and services traded in the marketplace. A nation or a region has many important products that are not traded in the marketplace and that, therefore, are not counted in the GNP or the GRP: for example, housing product—not new houses built or houses sold or rented, but the amount of adequate housing that was available for people and that they used. Similarly, one could think in terms of a national or regional health product, leisure product, nutrition product, job satisfaction product, environmental product, safety product, musical product, inventiveness product, or other personal and community products not traded in the marketplace. In terms either of the present level of welfare or of future prospects for growth and development, surely many noneconomic products are at least as important as economic products.

Then there is the problem that the monetary volume of economic product says nothing about the benefit or quality of that product or its implications for future development. A high money volume of product produced today may have been at the expense of efficiency, or of resources for tomorrow, or of slowly capturing a high-quality market that is dependable over the long run.

Third, there is no really good way of placing money value on the economic product. Economists like to tell the story of a woman who married her gardener and thereby reduced the GNP because she no longer purchased his services in the marketplace. But even within the marketplace, the same commodity probably sold for hundreds of different prices in different places in the nation or the region during a year. How is the real money value of a year's product to be counted in a meaningful way? Furthermore, the economic value of a thing expressed in GNP terms is its price in a free competitive marketplace. Most prices, however, are not determined by free competitive marketplace forces. They are administered by monopolies, governments, cartels, or others whose decisions are motivated by interests other than arriving at the free-market price. Moreover, even when there is a free market of sorts, there are interdependencies among prices that at times cause the relationship between a price and the economic value of a good to be somewhat obscure. For example, in periods of high interest rates, the prices of products normally purchased on credit will tend to be relatively depressed. Can one meaningfully say that this reflects a decline in their economic value?

With all that, regional income measures and income-and-product accounts have a useful role to play, along with other methods of analysis, by providing a view of the region from their unique perspectives.

THE STRUCTURE OF BASIC INCOME MEASURES

The basic income measures employed by analysts at the regional or local levels are, for the most part, counterparts of those commonly employed at the national level. They do not always have the same analytical usefulness, however, and because of data-collection difficulties, computation of regional income measures is generally more problematic. Figure 3.1 provides the conceptual structure of income measures.

Gross regional product is the total value, at market prices, of final goods and services produced in the region during the accounting year. The word final means that the goods and services are not purchased for further processing or resale within the region.

GRP can be computed by adding up personal consumption expenditures in the region, private investment in the region, local and central government expenditures in the region, and all sales of the region's products and services outside the region (regional exports), and then subtracting the value of goods and services purchased outside the region and resold in the region or used as inputs to the region's production (imports). One could also use total, not just regional, expenditures, of local persons, firms, and governments, plus all expenditures by foreigners in the region; but then imports would include all purchases by regional residents, firms, or agencies outside the region, not only those used for resale or as inputs. Alternatively, the value, at market prices, of final goods and services produced in the region by each industry category (less the value of imported inputs), or the value added by each industry category, could be summed to obtain the gross product of the region for the accounting year.

Figure 3.1 begins with GRP and deducts the various charges against it (the cost incurred in the production of goods and services). One of the costs of production is the using up of capital that must be replaced. When capital consumption allowances are netted out of gross regional product, the resulting figure is net regional product (NRP).

However, the value of goods and services at market prices is not identical with income to factors of production (land, labor, capital), because some of the costs of production (such as indirect business taxes) do not represent payments to economic factors. When all business payments other than those to factors of production are deducted and subsidies to enterprises in the region are added in, the resulting figure is regional income, which represents the actual earnings accruing to owners of the factors of production in the region in consequence of the production of gross regional product.

Regional personal income includes that part of regional income that people take home in the form of personal earnings from all sources before taxes. Thus, from regional income must be deducted social insurance contributions, corporate income taxes, retained corporate profits, and the like. But it also includes income from other sources, such as dividends, which must be added in.

FIGURE 3.1

Conceptual Structure of Income Measures

<u>Gross regional product</u> (at market prices)

less   capital consumption allowances of enterprises in the region

equals <u>net regional product</u>

less   business (including government enterprises) payments other than those to or on behalf of local factors of production

plus   subsidies to enterprises in the region

equals <u>regional income</u> (paid to local factors of production)

less   regional income not accruing to persons

plus   other income accruing to persons residing in the region

equals <u>regional personal income</u>

less   personal taxes paid by residents of the region

equals <u>regional personal disposable income</u>

less   personal consumption expenditures by residents of the region for subsistence

equals <u>regional personal discretionary income</u>

which
is used
for   regional personal savings and
        regional personal discretionary consumption

When personal taxes are deducted from regional personal income, the resulting figure is regional personal disposable income, the money people can spend. In many cases, however, people have payments due on commitments made previously. In the context of a poor region, commitments made previously might meaningfully include minimum subsistence expenditures, such as those for basic food and shelter. When these are deducted one arrives at regional personal discretionary income, the money people can save or spend as they please.

Regional per capita income is usually based on regional personal income or regional disposable income, and is simply income divided by population.

Any of these income measures can be computed by building up or by breaking down. Thus, the regional analyst can begin by estimating gross regional product by a building-up procedure involving estimation and then summation of the various expenditure or production components. He then proceeds to a breaking-down process in order to arrive at various income measures. Or he may do it the other way around and begin with disposable income or personal income estimates.

Two important income measures that cannot be arrived at through the scheme presented in Figure 3.1 are median family (or household) income and median family (or household) per capita income. The former is simply the midpoint in the array of all the family (or household) incomes in the region, such that 50 percent of the families have an income that is greater and 50 percent have an income that is lesser. The latter measure is computed by dividing the former by the region's average family (or household) size. This yields the income available to each member of the family or household with the median income.

Average family income has an analytical value that is identical with that of per capita income.

CONSIDERATIONS REGARDING
BASIC INCOME MEASURES

Gross regional product was discussed earlier. Suffice it here to add that the concept of analysis in terms of product and income is borrowed from analysis of business enterprises whose purpose is to produce product and earn income. Regional purposes, even regional economic purposes, may be broader than that. The point is that the GRP measures what GRP measures, and nothing more. That this be defined as "the market value of final goods and services produced in the region" does not make it so, nor does it ensure that it is comparable with GRP computed for other regions.

The same comments apply to net regional product. This measure is particularly useful in conjunction with gross regional product because a comparison of the two highlights the portion of the region's production that originates with capital consumption. In other words, the difference between gross regional product and net regional product represents a portion of revenues that will have to be allocated to capital replacement in order to maintain a constant level of output, if nothing else changes.

Both gross regional product and net regional product may be computed on a per capita basis. Such a computation provides an additional dimension to the analytical value of these measures for interareal and intertemporal comparisons. However, if the comparability of GRP or NRP figures for different areas is in question to begin with, conversion to a per capita basis does not improve the situation.

Regional income is an important measure because it represents the earnings of owners of local factors of production resulting from the parts they played in producing gross regional product. Accordingly, the change in regional income is a more accurate reflection than the change in GRP or NRP of the impact a change in regional production had on the earnings and welfare of the region's residents, both individuals and organizations. Again, the measure takes on added significance when compared with gross regional product and highlights the difference in the value of regional production in terms of revenues obtained in the marketplace, on the one hand, and the portion of those revenues accruing as income to local factors of production, on the other.

Regional personal income is of the utmost importance because it provides a more direct indication of the welfare of people. However, the welfare of people and economic development may not be one and the same thing, in the short run. A change in regional personal income is the net result of the participation of the human factor of production in a changing regional product and changes in income from sources unrelated to the region's production. Thus, an immigration of unemployed people into a region could result in an increase in regional personal income stemming from increased welfare payments or other public assistance. Without a knowledge of what is behind the increase, the measure can be quite misleading if used as an indicator of regional development, of prospects for long-run increases in personal welfare.

Regional personal disposable income provides an indication of individual command over goods and services, and is particularly useful as an interareal or intertemporal comparative indicator. A comparison of the changes in regional personal income and regional disposable income highlights the portions of the change in personal income available for public goods, on the one hand, and private goods, on the other. This can be of obvious importance in regional-development-policy decision making.

A change in income in a region is registered by changes in the incomes earned by people and by changes in the number of people earning incomes. The value of per capita income measures is that they register changes only when, and to the extent that, there is a disparity between the rate of growth in the region's income and the rate of growth in the region's population. It is, of course, entirely possible, over a given period, that income in a region may show impressive growth, while the population of the region may grow by an even greater proportion. In such a case, per capita income would

help reveal the true significance of the relative changes by register-
ing a decline for the period. While it provides some indication of
changes in individual welfare, per capita income does not provide the
analyst with any insight into the distribution of income. Thus, if income and population in a region were to remain unchanged over a period but there occurred a shift from a highly skewed income distribution to a relatively even one, per capita income would remain constant; and on the basis of this measure alone, the analyst would be
unaware of a development of major importance for the future of the
region.

Median family (or household) income provides an indication of
income distribution and how this distribution changes over time. It
becomes an exceptionally useful income measure when supplemented
by the maximum and minimum figures for the range of incomes in
the region. The type of survey upon which median family- or house-
hold-income estimates would be based could be designed to supply
information upon which total-income (and, therefore, per capita income) estimates could be based as well, with virtually no extra effort.

In many countries, substantial differences in average family
size have been found to exist among regions. Furthermore, many
regions have shown dramatic changes in average family size over relatively brief periods. Such factors would bring into question the
meaningfulness of median family (or household) income as a measure,
particularly for interareal or intertemporal comparisons. Median
family (or household) per capita income overcomes these possible ob-
jections in much the same way that per capita computations facilitate
more meaningful comparisons of regional disposable income and regional personal income.

Given the full array of regional income measures, the regional
analyst would still be less than entirely satisfied. There would be an
urge to delve deeper, to consider the disaggregated components of
the income measures, and through an analysis of the structure of the
economy, to draw conclusions concerning development issues. To this
end, he or she would seek the full set of regional income-and-product
accounts behind the income measures.

DEVISING A SET OF REGIONAL ACCOUNTS

The regional income-and-product accounts can be any set of
balanced accounts that cover the economic activity of the region, or
a component of that activity, in greater or lesser detail. They may
be organized along any desired lines in accordance with analytical
needs and data availability.

Generally, in devising a set of regional accounts, national accounting procedures serve as a starting point. The main justification

for this is that they are there, and they constitute a familiar and convenient double-entry accounting system. It would be useful for analytical purposes to have a set of regional accounts comparable to the
national accounts, but to accomplish this usually requires revision
of the national accounts in the image of those devised for the region,
for regional accounts generally cannot be meaningfully patterned precisely after national accounts.

First, the regional economy is usually considerably more open
than the national economy. This means that at the regional level
both parties to a transaction are less likely to reside in the same
economy. The conceptual and statistical implications of this are obvious. Second, while data collection for the national accounts is often
systematized, at the regional level equivalent data may be nearly impossible to obtain. This is so because record keeping at the regional
level is often virtually unknown, and also because of disclosure problems. Most important, national accounts are designed to provide an
analytical basis for national decision-making purposes. Key tools of
national policy, notably fiscal and monetary policy, are not found in
the regional developer's tool kit; so in devising a system of accounts,
the regional analyst has analytical objectives different from those of
his counterpart at the national level.

The first step, then, in devising a set of regional accounts is
to consider carefully what the analytical objectives of the accounts
are to be. In figuring out how to achieve these objectives through the
design of the accounts, the analyst should consider questions such as
the following: How can the accounts reflect and help throw light on
elements of major analytical importance to development considerations? How can relevant ethnic, sociocultural, administrative, and
other substructures be reflected in the accounts? How can relationships with the rest of the world be usefully but concisely examined?
What meaningful balancing devices can be employed? What types of
data are available? and How can these be organized and processed in
order to maximize their analytical usefulness?

SIMPLIFIED EXAMPLES OF REGIONAL ACCOUNTING

Imagine a region with the following characteristics:

1. All residents are farmers.
2. The total value of farm products for the year 19YY at local
market prices is Mu. 20 million (Mu. = monetary units).
3. Farm families have reported that, on the average, they retain 25 percent of what they produce for their own use and sell the
remainder.

4. There is an uninhabited marketplace in the region where all farmers sell their produce to merchants who come there to buy on traditional market days.

5. In this same marketplace residents of the region purchase their household and farmyard goods from dry goods merchants who also come there on traditional market days. There is no other expenditure outlet.

6. Both the produce merchants and the dry goods merchants live outside the region. The produce merchants take all the produce they purchase with them for resale outside the region. The dry goods merchants bring all their wares with them when they come to market, and they take what remains, along with their earnings, when they leave the region at the close of market days.

7. Of residents' purchases at the marketplace, 10 percent is for replacement investment.

8. All transactions in the marketplace are for cash.

9. There are no personal savings.

10. The government neither collects taxes nor spends money in the region.

If we follow the general rules and format of national income-and-product accounting, a set of accounts for our region, Region Z, might be designed in accordance with the illustration in Figure 3.2. In this set of accounts, regional income measures have been highlighted on the left side.

Available data have informed us that farmers retain Mu. 5 million of their produce and sell Mu. 15 million in the marketplace. Their earnings of Mu. 15 million are then used to purchase goods in the marketplace. Capital replacement purchases comprise Mu. 1.5 million of these expenditures. Thus, on the right side of the accounts in Figure 3.2, Mu. 1.5 million is registered as gross private regional investment. The remainder of the Mu. 20 million went for personal consumption expenditures in one form or another. Of this amount, goods worth Mu. 15 million were imported, and these imports were offset by an equal amount of exports, so that net exports amounted to zero. Government expenditures were also zero. On the left side of the accounts in Figure 3.2 the estimate of capital consumption allowances was based on actual spending for replacement investment.

When we force the accounts into a simplified national accounting framework, a picture is provided that enables comparison with the nation, perhaps, but it is not particularly useful for the regional analyst. First, even this simplified national format contains an excessive amount of unnecessary detail that may contribute to obscuring the essential information. Second, the accounts provide no indication of the rather important fact that one-quarter of farm production never

FIGURE 3.2

Income-and-Product Accounts for Region Z, 19YY
(in thousands of monetary units)

Regional Income and Other Charges against Gross Regional Product		Gross Regional Product	
Personal savings	0	Regional personal consumption expenditures	18,500
Personal consumption expenditures	18,500		
Subtotal: Personal disposable income	18,500	Gross private regional investment	1,500
Personal taxes	0		
Subtotal: Personal income	18,500	Government expenditures in the region	0
Transfer payments	0		
Undistributed profits	0		
Corporate income tax	0	Net exports	0
Subtotal: Regional income	18,500	Exports 15,000	
		Imports (15,000)	
Indirect business taxes	0		
Subtotal: Net regional product	18,500		
Capital consumption allowances	1,500		
Gross regional product	20,000	Gross regional product 20,000	

enters the monetized economy. Then, one might conclude from the accounts that capital consumption allowances are calculated on the basis of refined business practices. In other words, the way in which investment decision making works (when a piece of equipment breaks, the farmer goes to the marketplace to buy a new part) is not reflected in the accounts. In general, the accounts convey no real feel for the economy of the region. Indeed, the accounts in Figure 3.2 provide no indication that the region is exclusively agricultural.

FIGURE 3.3

Income-and-Product Accounts for Region Z, 19YY,
Modified Format
(in thousands of monetary units)

Gross Regional Income		Gross Regional Product	
Personal cash savings	0	Personal consumption expenditures	
Cash income used for farm capital replacement purchases	1,500	Imputed value of produce consumed on the farm	5,000
		Cash purchases	13,500
Cash income available for purchases of household and farmyard consumption goods	13,500	Gross private regional investment	
		Replacement investment	1,500
		Growth investment	0
Subtotal: Personal cash income	15,000		
Imputed income from sales of farm produce to self	5,000	Government expenditures	0
Income from nonfarm activities	0	Net exports	0
		Exports 15,000	
Income from all other sources	0	Imports (15,000)	
Taxes	0		
Gross regional income	20,000	Gross regional product	20,000

    If we use the national framework as a starting point, however, a set of accounts might be devised along lines illustrated in Figure 3.3. Here, the explicit shortcomings of the previous set of accounts have been overcome. The structure and operation of the primitive farm economy stand out relatively clearly. Even the zero entries have been thought out and contribute useful information about the region.

FIGURE 3.4

Income and Product of Residents, by Source and Use,
Region Z, 19YY, Simplified Format
(in thousands of monetary units)

Residents' Income		Residents' Product	
Income from exports	15,000	Value of farm prod- ucts	20,000
		For export 15,000	
Imputed income from sales of farm pro- duce to self	5,000	For local con- sumption 5,000	

Total residents'
    income
	20,000	Total residents'
		    product
			20,000

But the accounts are a highly flexible tool. The analyst may choose to minimize detail and emphasize a single aspect of the economy in which he or she is interested or to which attention should be drawn. The illustration in Figure 3.4 represents an approach to accounting for Region Z that emphasizes sources of income and uses of product of the region's residents. In this format, uses of income are not dealt with, and product is computed directly by industry category (in this case, there is only one), instead of through the summation of the expenditure categories to which it is equal.

FIGURE 3.5

Expenditures of and Purchases from Residents, by Origin,
Region Z, 19YY, Simplified Format
(in thousands of monetary units)

Residents' Expenditures		Purchases from Residents	
Imports	15,000	By rest of world	15,000
Local goods	5,000	By local residents	5,000

Total expenditures of
    residents
	20,000	Total purchases from
		    residents
			20,000

FIGURE 3.6

Regional Income and Product, with Explicit Locational Adjustment,
Region Z, 19YY, Simplified Format
(in thousands of monetary units)

Regional Income		Regional Product	
Farm income	20,000	Value of farm products	20,000
From imputed value of produce consumed on the farm	5,000	For home consumption	5,000
		For export	15,000
From cash sales to exporting merchants	15,000	Gross sales of merchants	15,000
		Consumption goods	13,500
		Capital goods	1,500
		Subtotal:	35,000
		(Less value of goods imported and earnings taken abroad by nonresident merchants)	(15,000)
Total income of region's residents	20,000	Total product of region's residents	20,000

Or the analyst may prefer to use an accounting framework other than income and product. In Figure 3.5 the data for Region Z have been organized according to expenditures of and purchases from residents of the region. In this case, detail has again been suppressed, and the analyst has emphasized the import-export features of the economy.

All the illustrations so far are based on the residence principle. That is, they are concerned with the region in terms of the resident population alone and not with the region as geographic space. They lose the locational import of the marketplace that is geographically within the region but economically outside it. This significant point might be registered in the accounts, as in Figure 3.6, by introducing the economic activity in the marketplace (to show that it is located in

the region), and then adjusting it out (to show that it is effectively outside the region).

If the region is viewed as a geographic unit alone, Mu. 35 million
of activity takes place. Accounts could be constructed on a geographic
basis alone, but this is generally not too meaningful. It is usually
meaningful and important, however, to compare the economy of the region as a geographic unit with the economy of the region as a population
unit. The simple import-export distinction may not provide an adequate reflection of the spatial significance of what has transpired. Figures 3.2 through 3.5 could have been constructed in the same way if
the marketplace had been located outside the region. In Figure 3.6
the basic data are the same, but information significant for the regional analyst that was obscured in previous illustrations has been
highlighted.

AN EXPANDED EXAMPLE OF REGIONAL ACCOUNTING

Figure 3.7 provides an illustration of regional accounts that follows a format very different from any of the previous illustrations.
Here, the accounts are concerned only with personal income, and particularly with personal income derived from current production in the
region.

Data on earnings have been collected at the paying establishments rather than at the earning households. Considerable detail on
earnings is provided in a double-entry framework, first by type of payments, and then by industry category.

In order to convert earnings paid by establishments in the region
into earnings of the region's residents, a net residence adjustment is
included. The negative residence adjustment figures show that the
earnings of residents who commute to work in the region exceed those
of the region's residents who commute to work outside the region. It
would be useful to have the residence adjustment disaggregated by inflows and outflows, by type of payment, and by industry category, but
detailed data of this sort are usually difficult to obtain. The residence
adjustment is generally arrived at by estimation techniques based on
sample data that seldom are adequate for disaggregated estimates.

Next, other types of income are added to total earnings of residents, and other adjustments are made in order to arrive at total personal income of residents of the region.

As a useful addendum to the accounts, per capita personal income is computed and indexed on national per capita income for the
two years.

If a similar set of accounts were supplied for the nation or some
other reference area, a very complete income picture of the region
would be provided in absolute and comparative terms.

FIGURE 3.7

Income Accounts for Region Q, 19XX and 19YY
(in thousands of constant monetary units)

	19XX	19YY
Earnings by type of payment		
Wages and salaries	650	1,750
Other labor income	15	50
Proprietors' income	110	200
Total earnings by type of payment	775	2,000
Earnings by industry category		
Farm	425	575
Nonfarm	350	1,425
Government	35	250
Central	30	175
Civilian	30	100
Military	0	75
Local	5	75
Private nonfarm	315	1,175
Manufacturing	110	635
Mining	5	5
Construction	40	100
Communication and transportation	35	80
Trade	70	175
Finance and related services	20	45
Other services and utilities	30	125
Other	5	10
Total earnings paid by Region Q establishment	775	2,000
Residence adjustment	(10)	(295)
Total earnings of Region Q residents	765	1,705
Property income	75	260
Transfer payments	20	75
Less personal contributions to social insurance	(5)	(50)
Total personal income of Region Q residents	855	1,990
Population (thousands)	57.5	80.5
Per capita income (monetary units)	15.0	25.0
Index: national per capita income = 100	60.0	85.0

The accounts shown in Figure 3.7 enable the regional analyst to answer or to suggest possible answers to a wide variety of questions of major importance to development planning, such as the following: What changes have taken place in the economic structure of the region over the period? What might have caused the basic structural changes? What have been the changing relative roles of the various types of income and the various sources of earnings? What change has taken place over the period in earnings of residents as a proportion of total earnings generated in the region? What change has taken place over the period in the relationship of per capita income to total earnings? How has the region fared in per capita income terms, relative to the nation?

Figure 3.7 is one of an endless variety of "correct" regional accounting methods. In some regions, for example, a breakdown of income by cultural groups might be more meaningful than earnings by type of payment. In many cases, it may be advisable to construct several different types of complementary accounts and take advantage of the unique benefits that each offers.

Further discussion on the use of income-and-product accounting in a regional planning context will be found in Chapter 8.

EXERCISES FOR CHAPTER 3

1. A regional analyst noted that the only new development in his region during the course of the year was the establishment of a new factory that employed 25 people at an average wage of Mu. 3,000 per year. Since this was the only change, he reasoned that the new level of regional income could be calculated by simply adding Mu. 75,000 to the prior year's regional income figure. The new per capita regional income figure could be calculated by simply adding 125 to the prior year's population figure (assuming that each worker brought with him the national average size family of five), and dividing the new income total by the new population total. Should the analyst be sent for more training, or should he be commended for devising a simple but reliable estimation technique? Why?

2. In the period 19XX-YY, the following changes took place in annual income indicators for a small rural region and for the country as a whole (in monetary units):

Income Increases	Region	Nation
Median household	30	320
Per capita	340	400
Median household per capita	115	110

What might have transpired over the period to bring these changes about?

3. Figures 3.2-3.6 are based on imaginary Region Z with a set of specific characteristics described in the text. Devise a set of accounts that reflects the information given, and then modify it where necessary to show the following changes in the region's characteristics (each change is to be considered separately):

a. The marketplace is outside the region instead of inside it.

b. One-third of the farmers' purchases in the marketplace is for consumer nondurables, one-third is for consumer durables, and one-third (instead of 10 percent) is for farmyard capital replacement goods.

c. Farmers store away 40 percent of what they retain for their own consumption and consume it the following year.

d. Of their revenues from sales of produce, farmers put an estimated Mu. 1 million in secret hiding places for use in emergencies.

e. The marketplace is once again located inside the region. Dry goods merchants live in the region and manufacture their wares there from local materials. They purchase from each other Mu. 1 million less than the farmers purchase from them, and they also purchase from the farmers Mu. 1 million of produce that formerly was sold for export. Of the dry goods merchants' purchases from each other, 10 percent are for capital replacement. The produce merchants continue to live outside the region and to export the produce.

f. Add a lumber mill and a furniture factory to the region's economy (let your imagination supply the Mu. figures representing their activities).

g. The government spends Mu. 500,000 in the region improving roads. This money is paid to local farmers who perform the work in the off-season. The region's residents pay Mu. 200,000 in taxes. Try the following variations:

The government is a central government
The government is a local government
Additional disposable income is spent in the marketplace
Additional disposable income is "spent" in savings

4. Consider Figure 3.7 and the discussion relating to it. Compute the percentage change for each entry over the period 19XX-19YY, the percent of total earnings paid by Region Q establishments represented by each entry in each year, and the change over the period in the percent of the total represented by each entry. For example, wages and salaries amounted to Mu. 650,000 in 19XX and Mu. 1,750,000 in 19YY. This represents a change of 169 percent over the period 19XX-19YY, 84 percent of total earnings in 19XX and 88 percent of the total in 19YY, and a change in percent of the total over the period of plus 4 percentage points. Numbers can be handled most easily by simply drawing four more columns on the table and filling in the computed figures for each entry. Once this is done, answer the interpretive questions posed in the text above (p. 48).

4

LINKAGES, FLOWS, AND REGIONAL BALANCE-OF-PAYMENTS STUDIES

There is a multitude of interregional linkages through which regions interact with each other. These interactions, in turn, generate impulses that work their way through the regional or local economy by means of an equally complex intraregional linkage system. The present chapter introduces several methods of examining interregional and intraregional linkages, both actual and potential, and the impact on the local economy, in balance-of-payments terms, of the region's interactions with the rest of the world.

Linkage studies are concerned with identifying potential flows. They seek to answer the question of how the region's actual or potential position within a set of interregional linkages can provide the bases for increasing the interregional and intraregional flows of goods and services to the benefit of the region's economy. This requires investigating several kinds of possible linkages: forward production linkages, involving further processing toward a finished product; lateral production linkages, a special form of forward linkage that goes to expanding an existing production process so that a broader array of outputs is produced from the same kinds of materials presently used as inputs; backward production linkages that involve moving closer to the basic inputs to a production process; distribution linkages that exploit the region's location in the interregional transportation network; commercial and service linkages that are oriented toward the region's potential retail trade and personal services trade areas; and other linkages, such as public service and institutional linkages. In order to provide a point of focus, the discussion in this chapter will concentrate on production linkages, but the comments made can be applied to other types of linkages as well.

Gravity studies attempt to determine the general inhibiting friction—or, viewed from a positive angle, the potential for greater interaction—among places or regions. The idea here is to provide a suggestion about the places to which flows might be increased and the possible ways for increasing them.

The final section of this chapter is concerned with balance-of-payments statements. These also deal with actual flows, but are not concerned with identifying their origins and destinations. Balance-of-payments statements focus on the money value of the flows that have taken place during the accounting year between the region and the rest of the world.

THREE SIMPLE LINKAGE INVESTIGATION DEVICES

There is no single general tool to apply in the investigation of linkages or linkage potentials. In fact, many of the methods of analysis discussed in other chapters of this book can provide clues to existing, potentially expanded, and potential new linkages. If the sole aim, however, is a preliminary linkage investigation, there are simpler, more direct, less expensive, quicker, and more easily performed methods that can be used.

One such device is the linkage survey. This is simply a survey of firms in various industry categories in the region as well as in other selected regions (and especially neighboring regions). It is conducted in order to uncover critical linkage aspects of the production process that might be exploited for regional development.

The exact survey technique most suitable is a matter for consideration in each particular case. If we recall the analyst's concern with both forward and backward production linkages, the information required falls into two major categories: that relating to outputs of the production process and that relating to inputs.

For any production process being investigated, the analyst would want to identify the outputs; determine how much, how, and where they are delivered; what they are used for; if they are intermediate goods, why they are not processed further; how the selling of the output is conducted; and basic price information. Inputs to the production process should be identified by quantities and unit money costs. Moreover, it would be good to know where the various inputs are obtained, how they are delivered, what they are used for, how they are processed, what substitutes are technologically acceptable, and how the firm conducts the buying of these inputs. Of course, this does not represent all the analyst might want to know about each production process investigated, but it does provide the basis for a set of lead questions for the survey.

A less direct but in some cases more informative technique involves an investigation of national input–output relationships. If a na-

tional input-output table is available, the forward and backward linkages of industries on a national basis can be studied for their rele-
vance to the potential expansion of the economic base of the region.
In the absence of national input-output tables, linkages of industries
actually or potentially represented in the region can be determined
by interviewing representatives of selected industries at the national
level and by reviewing industry trade journals. Often it will be found
that more valuable linkage information can be obtained at the national
level, because at this level a broader perspective on industry input-
output technologies is available and also because at this level the industry representative will generally have less fear of divulging trade
secrets.

Finally, the location quotient constitutes what is perhaps the
simplest of all devices for providing at least a first indication of
areas where more detailed linkage investigations are warranted. The
location-quotient technique involves a comparison of the extent to
which selected economic activities are found at the regional and national levels, relative to other activities to which they are linked.
For example, the number of square meters of floor space in cold
storage plants per hectare of vegetables and fruits grown by commercial farmers might be calculated and compared at the regional and
national levels. If the regional ratio is lower than that for the nation,
the possibility of unexploited regional linkage potentials may be hinted.
In calculating the ratio at the regional level, the denominator (hectares of vegetables and fruits in the above example) should encompass
the potential service area of the region, and it should not be restricted
or expanded simply to conform to the area defined by the given borders of the region.

There are a number of problems with the location-quotient technique. In the first place, the analyst must know something about the
production process before meaningful ratios can be computed. Then,
the implicit assumption in using the location quotient is that what is
found in the nation should and could be found in the region as well.
It must also be remembered that the region is part of the nation, and
therefore, it influences the national ratio. These and other problems
need not represent serious obstacles to the use of this technique for
exploratory purposes, however. Assistance from persons familiar
with various production processes is available for identifying meaningful ratios to be computed, and where appropriate, norms other
than the entire nation can be selected for comparison.

A fuller discussion of the location quotient appears in Chapter 5.

GRAVITY STUDIES

Gravity studies employ as a point of departure the proposition
that the intensity of potential interaction between two places varies

directly with their combined mass and inversely with the distance between them.

Imagine an isolated region with two cities, A and B, and a sprinkling of smaller towns of various sizes. Imagine further that the friction of distance among these places is zero—or put simply, that it costs nothing in time or money to travel. It would not be unreasonable to suppose that under such circumstances the amount of travel from, say, City A to any other place would be directly related to the size, or mass, of that other place. If we take population as the measure of mass, and City B as the other place, then the proportion of all the trips from City A that terminate in City B would be the same as City B's proportion of the population of the region (excluding the population of City A). The proportion of all the trips from City A that terminate in any other place would, of course, be calculated in the same way.

But of real interest are, in fact, the consequences of the friction of distance between places. This can be measured by finding out the actual proportion of all the trips from City A that terminate in City B and comparing that with the proportion calculated on the basis of mass alone. This comparison could be expressed as a friction ratio:

Effects of distance friction from A to B

$$= \frac{\text{Actual proportion of trips from A to B}}{\text{Hypothetical proportion of trips from A to B}}$$

Starting with this relatively simple idea, a structure of gravity-study analysis can be erected that is as simple or as complex as the analyst desires. The approach can be used to assess one type of interaction within one industry from one place to another, or it can be used to construct a generalized interaction map showing relative intensity of interaction among all major places in a region. The measure of mass need not be population but could be gross product, retail sales, employment, per capita income, units of market space, or any other measure appropriate to the analysis. In fact, a number of friction ratios can be calculated using alternate measures of mass as a means of trying to ascertain those that seem to matter most or that seem to be closely related, or for purposes of averaging and generalizing. Similarly, the measure of interaction need not be in terms of trips. It could be in terms of tons or value of a specific commodity that flows from one place to another in, say, a year, or it could be in terms of any other interaction of analytical interest. Or, a number of friction ratios can be calculated using alternate interaction measures.

And then, means can be devised for attempting to identify the relative significance of different measures of distance—in fact, different kinds of distance—that cause flow-inhibiting friction. Distance can be expressed as the actual distance along specific waterway, motor, railway, or other routes; it can be expressed in terms of the money/time cost required for travel; or it can be expressed in terms of red tape or other relevant measure. By comparing the friction ratios between a place and two other places equidistant in kilometers from it, for example, one could account for the difference in the friction ratios entirely in terms of other kinds of distance. By doing this with several sets of places, one could derive a relationship between kilometers of distance, on the one hand, and other kinds of distance, on the other, that could be applied to all friction ratios. One could use the same technique to isolate the effects of other kinds of distance. Obviously, there are many variations possible on this theme.

Gravity studies have clear usefulness in helping to understand what inhibits interaction or where there may be potentials for expanding it. They have equally clear limitations that must be taken into account. For one thing, the approach is based on a comparison of proportions. While statistical means for working with absolute numbers can be devised, none of them are really satisfactory for practical purposes. This means that the analyst can never really know to what extent the overall volume of interaction is inhibited, but must assume that the factors inhibiting the relative proportion of total interaction would be the same as the factors inhibiting the total volume of interaction. Such an assumption should be made very cautiously.

The fact that regions are open economies introduces obvious difficulties. The fact that for purposes of interregional (rather than interurban) gravity studies the region must be viewed as a single mass imposes limitations. Then there is the observation that the effects of any type of mass are probably not linear in reality. This means that the hypothetical proportion of interaction between two places is not really an independent variable and it cannot really be derived independently of distance; it truly is hypothetical. The significance of mass when two places are close together will be different from its significance when two places are very far apart. Finally, a limitation is created by the potential difficulty in obtaining just the right data. The actual structure of a gravity study that is designed for a region or local area will likely be as much a function of available or obtainable data as it is of analytical priorities.

This is not to cast dispersions on the usefulness of gravity studies. It is rather to place such studies in context, so that they can be made useful. Clearly, in designing a gravity study, the objective of the analysis must be sharply in focus, and it must be determined that the objective can be reasonably well achieved despite the limitations. The same can be said for every method of analysis.

FLOW STUDIES

Commodity flow studies identify by origin and destination the commodities and their quantities that flow to and from the region. Usually, origins and destinations are given in terms of regions or cities. Information of this sort can highlight important interregional linkages and provide a commodity picture of the region's role in the national fabric. Time-series information provided by flow studies conducted at regular intervals will provide insights into the shifts in import sources and export markets of the region and will give valuable clues to likely future developments. An analysis of data from flow studies can provide a basis for assessing the relative distance frictions of commodities exported by the region and clues to commodity and market combinations with the greatest potential. Thus, commodity flow studies provide data of immediate analytical value; they also are of value in providing input to other analysis techniques. In some cases, commodity flow studies have provided the basis for balance-of-payment statement estimates.

General commodity flow studies invariably base annual estimates on sample surveys. Complete counts may be possible only when the period of time or number of commodities covered by the study is very limited. Surveys can be conducted by direct counting techniques at the borders of the region or at origin and destination points in the region. Where a tradition of record keeping prevails, the survey can be conducted by indirect techniques.

However conducted, the objective of the survey is the gathering of information that enables the construction of tables (matrices) and maps showing the origins and destinations of at least major flows of specific commodities, by quantities. Table 4.1 provides an illustration of a commodity-flows matrix. The illustration should be considered as conceptual in nature because it is unlikely that much could be gained by providing all the information indicated in Table 4.1 in a single matrix.

More likely, commodity-flows information would be presented in a series of matrices and maps that could then provide greater detail in accordance with what the analyst deems worthy of emphasis. Greater or lesser detail may be provided by individual commodity; by commodity flows exceeding a certain weight, count, or money volume; by points of origin and destination; by flows exceeding or less than a specified distance; by mode of delivery; by a final or intermediate goods distinction; and so on.

Thus, the data from a general commodity flow study might be presented first in a matrix that listed the commodities or major commodities flowing interregionally that originated in the region by point of destination and those flowing into the region by point of origin. For

TABLE 4.1

Illustrative Commodity-Flows Matrix

Commodity Flows to and from Region Z, by Mode, 19YY[a] (Thousands of Monetary Units, FOB Value)	Region X	Region Y	Big City A	Big City B	Total	Other Countries[b]
Commodities, Origin Region Z						
Cart: Commodity 1						
Commodity n						
Truck: Commodity 1						
Commodity n						
Train: Commodity 1						
Commodity n						
Boat: Commodity 1						
Commodity n						
Totals: Commodity 1						
Commodity n						
All Commodities						
Commodities, Destination Region Z						
[Use same format as above]						

[a] Estimates for 19YY based on surveys conducted Tuesday of first full week of each month.

[b] No overseas port in Region Z. Shipments to or from other countries also counted in region or city through which shipped.

each, the annual volume of the flow by unit count, weight, or money
value would be indicated. This summary matrix could be followed
by others dealing in detail with commodity flows by mode of transportation, such as in Table 4.1; with commodities traveling over a specific distance range (for example, 50 kilometers or more); with
flows only between the region and a primary city; with commodities
having flow volumes over a certain weight (for example, 100,000 tons);
or other breakdowns that may be of special interest.

For special purposes, limited-scope flow studies may be adequate. Passenger, telephone, telegraph, or newspaper flow studies
can be undertaken, for example, to provide analysts and planners
with indications of centrality of urban places in their regions.

Conceptually, commodity flow studies present little problem.
In practice, however, their execution is not a simple matter. In the
first place, it will be found that obtaining complete information is a
most difficult task, particularly in regions where large volumes of
commodities flow across the borders in individually owned rather than
commercial carriers. When surveys are conducted so that the annual
estimates do not reflect seasonal irregularities, serious problems
may occur in terms of manpower availability and survey cost. Then,
too, it may be nearly impossible in some cases to distinguish between
commodity flows terminating in a particular region or city and those
that are only transferred to other carriers there. In general, as detail increases, so do the technical problems.

For various categories of funds, money flow studies provide the
same type of origin and destination information that commodity flow
studies provide for commodities. Money flow studies can complement
and provide a crosscheck to commodity flow studies. They can help
point up financial barriers to development, and they can provide valuable insights into interregional financial linkages among institutions.

However, such studies tend to be of little value unless done in
substantial detail. This detail requires a degree of monetization and
level of record keeping not usually found in poor regions. For this
and other reasons, money flow studies have often been found impracticable for such regions. In most cases, special purpose studies such
as credit-source studies or type-of-savings studies will satisfy the
needs of the analyst. Such studies must be devised in accordance with
needs, institutional environment, and data availability in each case.

BALANCE-OF-PAYMENTS STATEMENTS

Balance-of-payments statements are valuable as complements
to other studies, such as income and product accounts and flow studies,
and also have substantial analytical value alone. They can provide, at

a glance, a large quantity of flow information, and they enable analysis of the terms of trade and what has been called the net profitability of the region. The balance-of-payments statement provides the most comprehensive picture of the nature of the region's economic relations with the rest of the world. Balance-of-payments statements computed at regular intervals provide particularly useful time-series data.

In compiling the balance-of-payments statement, the regional analyst is confronted with problems of disclosure, inadequate records, and the like, which are confronted as a matter of course in regional studies, as well as some problems unique to balance-of-payments studies.

Balance-of-payments statements are drawn up in terms of money. This means that the analyst may have to obtain unit prices for the goods that flow in interregional trade in order to estimate money values on the basis of unit or weight volume data from commodity flow studies or other sources. Meaningful prices may be difficult to obtain because different prices are often quoted to different buyers, prices may change during the year, and some prices are quoted without transportation costs, or free on board (FOB), while others are quoted with cost, insurance, and freight (CIF) included.

It is often tempting to base estimates on national average prices for the year, but this can lead to gross misrepresentation in terms of the values of the flows at the region's borders. Of course, the ideal solution to the problem is to obtain annual reports on the money value of goods flowing in interregional trade from exporting and importing agents in the region. However, this solution requires that the bulk of commodities and services in interregional trade be handled by a limited number of agents, that these agents can be identified, that they keep records satisfactory for the purpose of the study, and that they cooperate in providing the information required. There are other problems, particularly with regard to capital flows, but solutions are very case-specific.

The objective of the balance-of-payments statement is to record the money value of inflows to and outflows from the region. The statement may deal with one or more specific types of flows, such as services or commodities, or it may record all flows. The precise structure of the balance-of-payments statement, the level of detail, the way in which the double-entry balance is brought about, the way in which various substructures of the region are highlighted, and so on, are matters for consideration in each individual case, in light of analysis objectives, data availability, and the resources available.

Ideally, it might seem that in constructing the balance-of-payments statement, the analyst would want to be able to identify each interregional transaction. This would require an inflow-outflow, double-entry accounting system based on the goods-flows principle.

FIGURE 4.1

Illustrations of the Double-Entry, Goods-Flows Accounting Concept

Example: Export of Mu.500 of grain in exchange for cash

Inflows		Outflows	
Cash (sales receipts)	Mu.500	Grain	Mu.500

Example: Export of Mu.500 of grain in barter exchange for sewing machine (based on market price of grain)

Inflows		Outflows	
Sewing machine	Mu.500	Grain	Mu.500

Example: Export of Mu.500 of grain in exchange for promissory note

Inflows		Outflows	
Short-term credit abroad	Mu.500	Grain	Mu.500

Example: Export of Mu.500 of grain in exchange for Mu.100 cash, a sewing machine, and a promissory note of Mu.200

Inflows		Outflows	
Cash (sales receipts)	Mu.100		
Sewing machine	Mu.200		
Short-term credit abroad	Mu.200	Grain	Mu.500

According to this principle, each movement of a commodity, service, debt paper, or cash is recorded in accordance with whether it is an inflow or an outflow. As Figure 4.1 illustrates, each interregional exchange would have both an inflow and an outflow aspect to it.

Let us turn to the fourth example of Figure 4.1. If the region exported Mu.500 of grain, this would be recorded as an outflow from the region by the goods-flows principle. And if, in exchange, the region received Mu.100 in cash, a sewing machine, and an IOU for Mu.200, these would be recorded as inflows to the region and would balance the outflow.

In practice, it is not possible to record each individual flow between the region and the rest of the world, nor is it really necessary to record or know this. Because earnings from exports pay for imports in general, what really concerns the analyst is the net or balance of payments rather than each individual payment and the exchange to which it is attributed.

The traditional balance-of-payments statement uses the payments-equivalent principle rather than the goods-flows principle. Under this principle, the net payments figure is arrived at through a system that classifies each inflow or outflow in accordance with the direction of the flow of the payment to which it typically gives rise.

A common format used in regional balance-of-payments accounting is patterned after that used at the national level. This format contains four major headings:

1. Current account: The current account shows the money value of goods, services, and transfers and gifts flowing in and out of the region during the period.

2. Capital account: The capital account shows long-term and short-term debt and equity purchased or sold during the current period. Capital movements may balance a current account entry or a cash movement.

3. Cash movements: These refer to bank demand deposits and currency (and, traditionally, gold) that move in or out of the region as the result of current account or capital account transactions. This may often have to be computed as a residual at the regional or local level.

4. Errors and omissions: Records on inflows and outflows are never complete, even at the national level. Thus, after careful, independent computation of the current account, the capital account, and cash movements, any imbalance that remains is attributed to errors and omissions. However, it may be independently estimated or computed as a residual.

Figure 4.2 provides a schematic representation of a regional balance-of-payments statement in a modified version of the national format. Three columns appear to the right of the item entries in this figure. The first, "Exports and Payments Inflows," records the money value of current and capital movements that result in new money flowing into the region. The second column, "Imports and Payments Outflows," records the money value of current and capital movements that result in payments by the region to the rest of the world. The third column provides the net balance for each of the four categories and, where desirable, for individual items. Thus, the inflow and outflow represented by each individual interregional exchange are not recorded as such in the balance-of-payments statement. Instead, all movements resulting in payments inflows are recorded separately, and all movements resulting in payments outflows are recorded separately.

The capital account and cash movements demonstrate how transactions on current account were financed. Thus, imbalance on cur-

FIGURE 4.2

Schematic Representation of a Balance-of-Payments Statement

Item	Exports and Payments Inflows (1)	Imports and Payments Outflows (2)	Net (1) − (2)
Current Account			
Commodities			
Commodity 1	Money value of goods exported	Money value of goods imported	
. . .			
Commodity n			
Services			
Tourism	Foreign tourist expenditures in region	Residents' spending abroad	
Transportation, financial, and other	Receipts from foreigners by local firms	Payments by residents to foreign firms	
Interest, dividends, other earnings, and transfers and gifts	Receipts from abroad by residents	Payments abroad by residents	
Totals on current account	Total (+)	Total (−)	Net balance (+ or −)
Capital Account			
Long term	Long-term commitments of residents to foreigners through foreign investment in the region, sales of equity and bonds abroad, and so on	Long-term commitments of foreigners to residents through residents' investment abroad, residents' purchases of equity and bonds abroad, and so on	
Short term	Short-term borrowings abroad	Short-term loans to foreigners	
Other			
Totals on capital account	Total (+)	Total (−)	Net balance (+ or −)
Cash Movements: Net movements of currency and demand deposits			(+ or −)
Errors and Omissions			(+ or −)

Note: "Foreign" and "abroad" refer to the rest of the world, including other regions of the country.

rent account must be offset by the net balance on capital account and
net cash movements. Cash movements represent the residual imbalance from current account and capital account net balances.

In some regions the capital account, or certain items in it, may
be impracticable or irrelevant. In such cases, a revision of accounting procedures will be necessary. One possibility is to record values
for those capital-account items that are relevant and obtainable, and
replace cash movements with a residual account entitled "Cash and
Debt Residual." In the extreme case, accounting could be provided
for current account only, with everything else a residual.

The example data of Figure 4.1 will aid in illustrating how the
balance-of-payments statement format of Figure 4.2 would work. In
the current account, the export of grain amounting to Mu. 500 would
be entered in column 1, as if a money inflow had already taken place
as a result of the export. An import of sewing machines of Mu. 200
value would also be entered in the current account, in column 2, as
if there had been a money outflow in payment. Thus, the net balance
on current account would be +Mu. 300. In the capital account, opposite
the item "short-term loans," Mu. 200 would appear in column 2 as if
there had been a money outflow in order to purchase (import) the debt.
Thus, the net balance on capital account would be Mu. 200. When the
net balances on current account and capital account are added together,
it is found that there remains +Mu. 100 of the +Mu. 300 imbalance on
current account that is not covered by the net balance on capital account. Therefore, +Mu. 100 must have been the net cash movement
and would be entered as in column 3. Figure 4.3 shows how the entries would appear.

The balance-of-payments statement based on the payments-
equivalent principle, as illustrated in Figures 4.2 and 4.3, has an
aesthetic imperfection in that the net column does not add to zero.
This is because the cash movement residual reflects the net imbalance
in the other accounts. Many analysts have seen fit to overcome this
by replacing "cash movements" with "cash outflow," with the result
that a net cash inflow takes on a negative sign and the net column adds
to zero.

In computing the accounts, many items may cause some confu-
sion at first. In general, it can be determined whether a particular
value belongs in column 1 or in column 2 by carefully considering
whether the effect is equivalent to a payment inflow or a payment outflow. For example, the excess of taxes paid to the central government over central government expenditures in the region would be entered in column 2 because it is a net money outflow. Recorded individually, rather than net, taxes paid out are a payment outflow, and
government expenditures are a payment inflow to the region.

The point must be emphasized that the balance-of-payments
statement may be designed along lines deemed most suitable by the

FIGURE 4.3

Sample Entries for the Balance-of-Payments Statement
(in monetary units)

Item	Exports and Payments Inflows (1)	Imports and Payments Outflows (2)	Net (1) − (2)
Current account			
Grain	500	0	
Sewing machines	0	200	
Totals on current account	+500	−200	+300
Capital account			
Short-term loans	0	−200	
Totals on capital account	0	−200	−200
Cash movements (residual imbalance)			+100
Errors and omissions			0

regional analyst in each particular case, as long as the basic account-ing principles adopted are sound and are adhered to consistently. In-deed, the net exports entry in the income and product accounts can be viewed as a primitive and incomplete form of the balance-of-payments statement. The analyst can start with this and expand in stages to the full-fledged balance-of-payments statement.

Further discussion on the use of balance-of-payments state-ments in a regional planning context will be found in Chapter 8.

EXERCISES FOR CHAPTER 4

1. Construct a balance-of-payments statement for Region W based on the following information for 19YY:

a. Records are extremely good because transactions are in a limited number of sectors only. Errors and omissions, of course, cannot be known. However, a study of historical data has shown that records in any year tend to err by 5 percent of current totals (verified by subsequent studies).

b. Region W exported Mu. 100,000 in cotton and Mu. 150,000 in rice in 19YY.

c. There is a small consumer-goods industry in Region W, which in 19YY, supplied 10 percent of local consumer nondurable purchases of Mu. 50,000. This amount (the 10 percent) comprised 50 percent of the industry's total sales.

d. All capital goods (amounting to only Mu. 10,000 in 19YY) that were purchased by Region W were of a primitive type and were manufactured locally. Actually, most of the Mu. 10,000 is imputed value of homemade farm implements.

e. There is no local consumer-durables industry, but all such products are sold through local agents. These agents recorded sales of Mu. 75,000 at wholesale prices in 19YY. (They refused to reveal the amount of overall markup on these goods.)

f. Records show that the Mu. amounts for exported and imported goods (with the exception of consumer durables) do not reflect delivered price, as they are derived from farm and factory price lists that are so-called factory-door prices (FOB factory). The full CIF price (cost, insurance, and freight) is an average of 3 percent higher; insurance and freight are always handled by firms local with respect to origin of the goods. Consumer durables are excluded, because for these, the price includes delivery by factory-owned vehicles.

g. Foreign ownership of farms and other enterprises in Region W received payments amounting to 30 percent of gross export sales in 19YY.

h. Rent and other income received by residents of Region W from property and debt owned elsewhere was Mu. 3,000 in 19YY.

i. Residents of Region W spent Mu. 15,000 while touring other parts of the country for business and pleasure in 19YY, while non-residents spent Mu. 2,000 in Region W for the same purposes in the same year.

j. Former Region W residents who moved to metropolitan areas sent Mu. 25,000 to help their families back home in 19YY. But Region W residents sent twice as much to relatives in regions where they were even more in need.

k. The local government is confined by law to an operating budget only. Thus, with no difficulty, it balances this budget perfectly every year.

l. There were no private savings in 19YY, and there seldom are in Region W, except in the form of the purchase of equity and debt from other regions. In 19YY Region W residents purchased no equity abroad, but they did purchase Mu. 5,000 in bonds and Mu. 5,000 of short-term debt from residents and enterprises in other regions. No equity, bonds, or loans were sold by residents of Region W to other regions in 19YY (nor to themselves, for that matter, since no enterprises were created or expanded, and household credit was available locally on an informal basis).

m. The central government collected taxes amounting to Mu. 40,000 from Region W, and it returned Mu. 15,000 in the form of infrastructure development and certain services in 19YY.

2. On the basis of the balance-of-payments statement you have constructed for the exercise above, as well as other information given above, list some of the important observations you might make, as a regional development practitioner, concerning Region W. What changes in what items would you hope to see over time as development progresses?

5

RELATIVE REGIONAL INDUSTRIAL-COMPOSITION ANALYSIS

The term <u>industry</u> as used here and elsewhere in this book means "branch of economic activity," and should not be confused with "manufacturing."

What is the industrial composition of the region? How does it compare with that of the country or of other regions? How is it changing? Which changes should be accommodated, and which discouraged? What changes should be stimulated? Mix-and-share, location-quotient, and related techniques provide means of understanding the industrial composition of the region, evaluating it in relative terms, and identifying possibilities for the expansion of various industries in the region. All this, of course, from the point of view of the region or local area, not the nation or the firm. Mix-and-share analysis focuses on the changes that have taken place in the industrial composition of the region; the location quotient is a shortcut tool for gauging regional specialization and expansion potentials.

MIX-AND-SHARE ANALYSIS

The change in regional employment relative to the change in national employment over a period can be viewed as the net of three effects. The first reflects the impact on the region of the change in total employment nationally. The second effect stems from the industry mix in the region, that is, the distribution of regional employment among higher- and slower-growth industries, relative to the industry mix prevailing nationally. The third effect relates to changing regional shares of total national employment in each industry. The notions of industry mix and regional shares are compared with the help of a diagram in Figure 5.1.

FIGURE 5.1

Diagrammatic Representation of Mix–and–Share Concepts

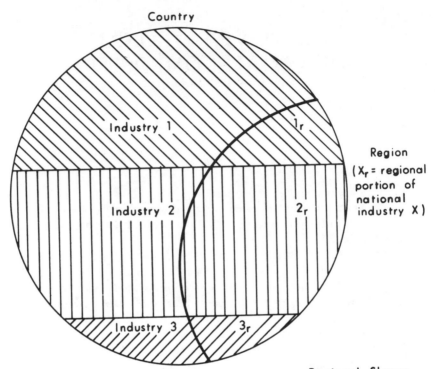

Country

Industry 1

1_r

Industry 2

2_r

Region
(X_r = regional
portion of
national
industry X)

Industry 3

3_r

Industry Mix

$$\frac{1_r}{1_r+2_r+3_r}, \ \frac{2_r}{1_r+2_r+3_r}, \ \frac{3_r}{1_r+2_r+3_r}$$

relative to

$$\frac{1}{1+2+3}, \ \frac{2}{1+2+3}, \ \frac{3}{1+2+3}$$

Regional Shares

$\frac{1_r}{1}, \ \frac{2_r}{2}, \ \frac{3_r}{3}$ at the

start of the period,
relative to

$\frac{1_r}{1}, \ \frac{2_r}{2}, \ \frac{3_r}{3}$ at the

end of the period

TABLE 5.1

Hypothetical Changes in National and Regional Employment,
19XX-YY
(absolute numbers in thousands)

| Industry | Employment | | Employment Change, 19XX-YY | |
| | 19XX | 19YY | Absolute | Percent |
	(1)	(2)	(3)	(4)
Nation				
Agriculture	10,000	10,000	000	00
Manufacturing	5,000	10,000	+5,000	+100
Services	6,000	9,000	+3,000	+50
Government	3,000	7,000	+4,000	+133
Total nation	24,000	36,000	+12,000	+50
Region Z				
Agriculture	150	120	-30	-20
Manufacturing	50	80	+30	+60
Services	50	95	+45	+90
Government	10	20	+10	+100
Total				
Region Z	260	315	+55	+21

Mix-and-share analysis provides a descriptive explanation of the change in regional employment over a period. It does this by isolating the individual components of change reflecting the national-growth effect, the industry-mix effect, and the regional-shares effect. The formula $R = N + M + S$ (where R is the total change in regional employment and N, M, and S are the individual components of change reflecting the national-growth, industry-mix, and regional-shares effects, respectively) provides the basis for mix-and-share analysis.

Suppose the changes in employment in a nation and in one of its regions, Region Z, over the period 19XX-YY, are represented by the data in Table 5.1. Total employment in the nation grew by 50 percent over the period, while total employment in Region Z grew by only 21 percent, less than half the national rate. How can the difference be explained?

By how much would regional employment have grown had each of its industries and, therefore, the regional total grown at the same rate as employment nationally? Table 5.2 shows the individual industry and total computations for N, the national-growth effect.

TABLE 5.2

National-Growth Effect, Region Z, 19XX-YY
(all figures in thousands)

Industry	Employment 19XX (1)	N = (1) National Growth Rate (0.50) (2)	R = Actual Growth (3)	R - N = M + S = Net Relative Change to Be Accounted For (4)
Agriculture	150	+75	-30	-105
Manufacturing	50	+25	+30	+5
Services	50	+25	+45	+20
Government	10	+5	+10	+5
Total Region Z	260	+130	+55	-75

Column 2 shows that when regional employment in each industry in the base year is multiplied by the national rate of growth (which is the same as the average rate of growth among industries nationally) over the period, it is found that 130,000 new jobs in Region Z can be attributed to a regional reflection of growth in national employment.

TABLE 5.3

Industry-Mix Effect, Region Z, 19XX-YY
(absolute numbers in thousands)

Industry	Distribution of Total 19XX Employment (in percent) Nation (1)	Region (2)	Deviation: Industry Growth Rate Minus National Growth Rate (in percent) (3)	Employment 19XX (4)	M = (3) × (4) (5)
Agriculture	42	58	-50	150	-75
Manufacturing	21	19	+50	50	+25
Services	25	19	0	50	0
Government	12	4	+83	10	+8
Total	100	100	0	260	-42

But actual growth in Region Z amounted to only 55,000 new jobs over the period. Hence, something transpired in the regional economy to offset the national-growth effect by 75,000 jobs. Since R = N + M + S, then M + S = R - N. Thus, the net relative change of minus 75,000 jobs by which the region grew more slowly than the nation can be accounted for by the industry-mix and regional-share effects.

What was the industry-mix effect? To what extent is the regional deviation from the national growth rate attributable to a regional industrial composition weighted, more than the nation, by industries with growth rates below the national average? Table 5.3 supplies the answer. The numbers in column 3 represent the individual industry deviations from the national growth rate. The deviations were computed by subtracting the national growth rate (in this case, 50 percent) from industry growth rates in the upper half of column 4 of Table 5.1, the original data. These deviations are then multiplied by regional employment in the respective industries in the base year. In this way, regional employment in each industry in the base year is weighted by individual national industry deviations from the national (average) growth rate. The results of these computations, column 5 of Table 5.3, represent the regional industry-mix effect.

Table 5.3 shows that the industry-mix effect was negative in the case of Region Z. Columns 1 and 2 confirm that in the base year the industry with a rate of growth below the national average, agriculture, represented a higher proportion of total employment in the region than in the nation. The other industries, which grew at rates equal to or greater than the average, represented smaller proportions of total employment in the region than in the nation. The result was a negative industry-mix effect that offset the national-growth effect by 42,000 jobs.

The regional-shares effect remains to be computed for Region Z. Since R = N + M + S, the regional-shares effect can be calculated residually as S = R - N - M, or 55 - 130 - (-42) = -33. In other words, the regional-shares effect can be computed as that part of the net relative change (in this case, minus 75,000 jobs) that was not accounted for by the industry-mix effect. This residual can be computed for each industry separately.

If each entry in the lower half of column 1 of Table 5.1 is divided by its counterpart in the upper half, and if the same is then done for column 2 of Table 5.1, a comparison of the results will confirm the regional-shares effect computations. It will be found that regional shares of agriculture, manufacturing, and government declined in Region Z between 19XX and 19YY. Only in the case of the services industry did the regional proportion of total national employment increase.

TABLE 5.4

Employment and Components of Employment Change, Region Z,
19XX–YY
(thousands of persons employed)

| | | | | Components of Employment Change | | |
| | | | | | | |
Industry	19XX (1)	19YY (2)	R Change 19XX–YY (3)	N National–Growth Effect (4)	M Industry–Mix Effect (5)	S Re–gional–Shares Effect (6)
Agriculture	150	120	–30	+75	–75	–30
Manufacturing	50	80	+30	+25	+25	–20
Services	50	95	+45	+25	00	+20
Government	10	20	+10	+5	+8	–3
Total	260	315	+55	+130	–42	–33

Summary mix-and-share data can be presented in a table such as Table 5.4. It presents the data in terms of absolute numbers only, but columns 3 through 6 could be presented in terms of percentages as well.

The analyst who compiled Table 5.4 and the previous tables might have provided an interpretive analysis of the agricultural sector in Region Z for the period 19XX–YY as follows:

Had the national agricultural sector grown at the national growth rate, and had regional employment in agriculture reflected this same growth rate, the number of jobs in agriculture in Region Z would have grown by 75,000, from 150,000 in 19XX to 225,000 in 19YY. Instead, however, regional employment in agriculture declined by 30,000 jobs, to 120,000 in 19YY. The gap between 225,000 and actual employment of 120,000 in 19YY, a net relative change of minus 105,000 jobs over the period in Region Z, can be accounted for by two factors. First, employment in the national agricultural sector grew by much less than national total employment, which grew by 50 percent; indeed, it did not grow at all. Because it grew more slowly than the national average, agricultural em-

ployment decreased as a proportion of the national total.
A larger proportion of the region's total employment was
in agriculture in 19XX than was the case nationally. Thus,
the relative decline experienced by this industry nationally
affected the region more severely than the nation and was
responsible for a relative loss of 75,000 jobs. Second,
during the period 19XX-YY, the region's share of employment in agriculture nationally declined. This decline
expressed itself as a relative decrease of 30,000 jobs in
Region Z over the period. Hence, the net impact of industry-mix and regional-share effects offset the national-
growth effect of plus 75,000 jobs by a net relative change
of minus 105,000 jobs; the region therefore experienced a
decline of 30,000 in agricultural employment.

Interpretations along similar lines could be provided for each of the
other industries and for total employment in the region.

In the above illustration of mix-and-share analysis, the regional economy was divided into four industry categories, and employment data that covered a single period were used. This represents
an application of the mix-and-share technique in its most limited
form. Mix-and-share analysis can be performed as well for subregions and towns in the study region. In certain cases, it may be appropriate to employ a reference area other than the nation, such as
a "parent" region, state, or province of which the study region or
local area is a part. The industries into which the economy is divided for purposes of the analysis may be as disaggregated as available data permit, even to the level of individual crops or products,
and all industries need not be at the same level of disaggregation.
In the Region Z illustration, for example, the analyst might have included a breakdown of agriculture by major crops. The analysis can
be performed for several historical periods, and it will always yield
greater insights when performed for several shorter periods rather
than for a single, longer, time span. Employment is most often used
as the unit of measure because it is generally the most available in a
form suitable for mix-and-share analysis. For certain purposes,
however, value added, gross revenues, sales, or some other output
or earnings measure can be used instead of employment. When a
money measure is used in addition to employment, the analysis may
provide insights concerning relative productivity impacts.

The mix-and-share technique can contribute to regional analysis in many ways. It points up with great clarity those industries for
which further detailed study is essential. Mix-and-share analysis
provides an overall picture of the role that the region has been play-
ing in the national industrial complex, and in combination with other

studies, it is a powerful tool for pinpointing relationships between the growth of the region's industries and overall national growth. If national projections by industry are available, the tendencies uncovered through mix-and-share analysis can aid in using them as a basis for projections of regional industries. Mix-and-share analysis can provide insights into the factors behind observed changes in the region's population and in other growth indicators. In helping the analyst understand the forces that brought the region to its present state and where it is likely to go from this state, mix-and-share analysis can provide a basis for preliminary development policy decisions regarding the region's industrial composition.

Mix-and-share analysis may raise as many questions as it answers. This follows, among other things, from its ability to focus on only a single variable at a time. For instance, in the Region Z illustration, the analysis concentrated on employment, while value added, investment, public spending, and other factors perhaps critically related to the region's industrial composition were ignored. In fact, the use of employment as the unit of measure results in a systematic understatement of the overall growth impact of industries undergoing the most rapid labor productivity gains. Furthermore, the analysis does not account explicitly for unemployment, and it remains for the analyst to relate data on changes in unemployment to the findings of the mix-and-share analysis. As in all analysis models, the source and quality of data used, the choice of base and terminal years, and the level of industry aggregation all seriously influence the results.

Finally, it must be reemphasized that mix-and-share analysis is a descriptive tool only. As such, it does not explain why a particular industry mix prevailed in the base year, why different industries experienced different growth rates nationally, or why changes in regional shares of national industries took place. Nor does it evaluate whether the changes that took place were desirable or undesirable. It will be noted, for example, that a decline in the regional share of an industry that is experiencing a relative decline nationally produces a double negative impact in terms of net relative change. The negative employment impact, however, may imply a shifting of workers from slow- to high-growth industries that may be very desirable from the standpoint of long-term regional growth. Hence, mix-and-share analysis has the potential to make a substantial contribution to overall regional analysis and to regional development policy. It is essential, however, that the analyst remain mindful of its limitations when making the transition from statistical results to interpretive analysis.

THE LOCATION QUOTIENT

In its most common form, the location quotient (LQ) is a device for gauging the relative specialization of a region in selected industries. The unit of measure often used is employment. Employment in a selected industry is related to a reference variable, usually total employment, at the regional and national levels. The findings at the two levels are then compared.

Employment in a selected industry is related to total employment by means of a simple ratio computation, and the ratios at the regional and national levels are compared by means of another ratio computation: the location quotient is a ratio of ratios. Following are two alternative formulas, arithmetic equivalents, for computing a location quotient.

$$LQ = \frac{\dfrac{X_r}{RV_r}}{\dfrac{X_n}{RV_n}} = \frac{X_r \text{ as a fraction of } RV_r}{X_n \text{ as a fraction of } RV_n}$$

or

$$LQ = \frac{\dfrac{X_r}{X_n}}{\dfrac{RV_r}{RV_n}} = \frac{X_r \text{ as a fraction of } X_n}{RV_r \text{ as a fraction of } RV_n}$$

where

X_r = employment in industry X in the region
X_n = employment in industry X in the nation
RV_r = reference variable value for the region
RV_n = reference variable value for the nation

An illustration of the computation of a location quotient is given in Figure 5.2, which uses data for 19XX from Table 5.1.

The arithmetic nature of the location quotient leads to the following rules of location quotient evaluation:

$LQ > 1$: If the location quotient is greater than 1, the region is more specialized than the nation in the study industry.

$LQ < 1$: If the location quotient is less than 1, the region is less specialized than the nation in the study industry.

$LQ = 1$: If the location quotient is equal to 1, the region and the nation specialize to an equal degree in the study industry.

FIGURE 5.2

Illustration of Location Quotient Computation
(in thousands)

$$LQ = \frac{\dfrac{150}{260}}{\dfrac{10,000}{24,000}} = \frac{0.58}{0.42} = 1.38$$

where

	Employment in Agriculture	Total Employment (reference variable)
Region Z	150	260
Nation	10,000	24,000

From this it follows that if a broad aggregate, such as total employment, is used as the reference variable, a regional export industry would be expected to have a location quotient greater than 1; a regional import industry would be expected to have a location quotient less than 1; and a local service industry would be expected to have a location quotient equal to 1. If the analyst finds that this is not the case, it should be of interest and importance to find out why.

The location quotient was presented above in its simplest form A time series of location quotients can be computed for relative trend detection; location quotients can be computed for subregions and towns in the study region; and employment can be considered at any level of disaggregation, down to a specific crop or product, in accordance with analysis needs and data availability. In some cases, it may be appropriate to employ a reference area other than the nation, such as a parent region or province, a median or average of other regions, the nation exclusive of the study region, or even a group of linked nations.

The specialization variable (the X variable representing the study industry in the formula) and the reference variable need not be in the same terms. When the specialization variable is employment in a selected industry, total employment is but one of many possible reference variables that might be chosen in accordance with the orientation of the analysis. If, for example, the industry under study is a service industry, and the location quotient is to be used as an indicator of adequacy of service, the appropriate reference variable might be population. If the service is oriented to households rather than individuals and the service characteristically has an inelastic demand, number of households might be the appropriate reference variable. If demand is elastic, median household income might be the appropriate reference variable. When the analysis is oriented toward productivity considerations, revenues, value added, or unit output measures could serve as reference variables. When using the location quotient as a tool in linkage investigations, employment or output in a linked industry might be appropriate reference variables.

In fact, the location quotient technique can be used to gauge relative specialization in any sense and by any units of measure deemed appropriate. Location quotients have been computed using movie theater seats as the specialization variable and 1,000 persons as the reference variable. In Chapter 4, an example of the location quotient was given in which square meters of floor space in cold storage plants was the specialization variable, and hectares of vegetables and fruits grown by commercial farmers was the reference variable. Where it is desirable that the region reflect reference area proportions, the location quotient can be set equal to 1, and the equation can be solved for the desired value of the specialization variable.

Moreover, the location quotient technique can help highlight regional relative inefficiencies, can assist in focusing on potential import substitutes or products with export expansion potential, and can provide an indication of industries for which further detailed study is most warranted. The location quotient has been found useful within the framework of linkage analysis, gravity studies, economic-base analysis, input-output analysis, mix-and-share analysis, and more. Because of its simplicity, the location quotient can be computed many times, relative to many reference variables, time periods, and reference areas, with a minimum investment in analysis time, manpower, and money.

In fact, the location quotient has been found so handy that an entire family of related measures has been developed for various specialized purposes. References will be found in the literature to measures such as the coefficient of localization, coefficient of specialization, index of diversification, coefficient of redistribution, coefficient of geographic association, coefficient of participation, index of occupational discrimination, coefficient of deviation, friction ratio, and more. All of these amount to little more than imaginative applications of the basic location quotient technique, computing a ratio of ratios, in response to particular analytical needs. Even mix-and-share analysis can be understood ultimately to be a sophisticated application of the location quotient approach.

Unfortunately, the ease with which the location quotient is computed can lead to its overuse and to an overstatement of its significance. It is, at best, a rough, descriptive indicator. Results of location quotient computations will be seriously influenced by the level of disaggregation of the specialization variables selected, the choice of reference variables, the choice of reference areas, and the choice of years for which it is computed. It will be found, too, that a location quotient computation produces results of inconsistent significance for different industries. Furthermore, the caveats implicit in any interareal comparison apply as well to the location quotient. Interareal differences in tastes and needs, levels of income, family sizes, exploitable resources, labor practices, and, therefore, economic structure require that statistical results of location quotient computations receive cautious analytical interpretation.

EXERCISES FOR CHAPTER 5

1. Suppose a feasibility study indicated that a vegetable canning factory could profitably be located in a certain region specializing in vegetable crops.

a. Identify the types of income impacts that might be direct, indirect, and induced if such a factory were established there.

b. Briefly describe the kinds of income impacts the region can expect in the short run and in the long run through linkage effects.

2. Complete the interpretive analysis of the mix-and-share example from the text. There remained to provide policy recommendations for agriculture and to provide analysis and policy recommendations for manufacturing, services, government, and the total region. What additional studies would you suggest for Region Z toward providing a basis for a regional development strategy?

3. Perform a mix-and-share analysis based on the following information (in thousands) for three industries selected for special study because of their dominance in Region K.

	Employment			
	Country		Region K	
Industry	19XX	19YY	19XX	19YY
Food processing	10	15	10	12
Wood products	30	25	5	8
Tourist crafts	5	8	3	4
Total for study industries	45	48	18	24

4. Provide an interpretive analysis and identify policy issues based on the results of exercise 3.

5. Suppose the data in exercise 3 represent the entire manufacturing sector in Region K but only 50 percent of the national manufacturing total, for both years.

a. What is the location quotient for the study industries as a whole and individually, for the region, for each year (total manufacturing employment is the reference variable)?

b. What is your interpretive analysis of the results?

c. What other reference variables might be employed to probe more deeply?

d. On the basis of the results, what detailed studies would you recommend for Region K?

6

ECONOMIC-BASE
ANALYSIS

Underpinning economic-base analysis is economic-base theory. The heart of economic-base theory is the proposition that the economic growth of a region, local area, or city depends upon exogenous demand. More precisely, whether a region grows or declines and the rate of growth or decline is determined by how it performs as an exporter to the rest of the world.

Exports to the rest of the world may be in the form of goods and services, including labor, that flow out of the region to buyers. Or they may be in the form of expenditures by foreigners in the region on goods and services that are immobile, such as those connected with the geography, climate, culture, historical significance, or relative location of the region. The export industries constitute the economic base, or basic sector, of the region or local area.

Employment and income in the basic sector are a function of exogenous demand, that is, outside demand for the exports of the region. However, numerous supporting activities are necessary to service workers in basic industries and their families, as well as the basic industries themselves. Of course, workers in the supporting activities service themselves and their own activities as well. The supporting activities, such as trade, personal services, and production for local markets, together comprise the nonbasic sector.

Both sectors, then, are related to exogenous demand—the basic sector directly and the nonbasic sector indirectly by supporting the basic sector. If exogenous demand for the exports of the region increases, the basic sector expands. This, in turn, generates an expansion in the supporting activities of the nonbasic sector. Economic-base theory holds that all economic activity can be classified as basic or nonbasic. Thus, basic employment (or income) plus nonbasic employment (or income) equals total employment (or income). The basic sector can be thought of as the regional exchange economy activity, and the nonbasic sector as the regional use economy activity.

THE BASE MULTIPLIER

The ratio of basic employment (or income) to nonbasic employment (or income) is called the economic base ratio. If, in a particular region, for every basic worker there are two nonbasic workers, the base ratio would be 1:2. If the base ratio is 1:2, then for every new job in the basic sector, two new jobs will be created in the supporting activities of the nonbasic sector. Similarly, for every decline of one job in the exporting activities of the basic sector, two jobs will go out of existence in the nonbasic sector.

If the base ratio is 1:2, the economic base multiplier is 3; when basic employment increases by one, a total of three new jobs, including both basic and nonbasic, will have been created. By multiplying the change in the basic sector by the base multiplier, an estimate of the total impact on the regional economy that results from a change in demand for basic goods can be computed.

The base multiplier is the sum of the two components of the base ratio with the basic component set equal to 1. An arithmetically equivalent formula for computing the base multiplier is the following:

$$\text{Base multiplier} = \frac{\text{Total employment}}{\text{Basic employment}}$$

The formula is given in terms of employment, but it could as readily have been expressed in terms of income or some other money measure.

From the formula for the base multiplier follows the formula for using the base multiplier to estimate total employment, given basic employment.

$$\text{Total employment} = (\text{Base multiplier})(\text{Basic employment})$$

If only the change in employment is of concern, essentially the same formula can be used.

Change in total employment

$$= (\text{Base multiplier}) (\text{Change in basic employment})$$

THE ECONOMIC-BASE STUDY

On the surface, the steps involved in an economic-base study appear relatively simple. First, a unit of measure is chosen. Most commonly employment is used because of its availability. Employment as a unit of measure also has the advantage of facilitating ready conversion of the results of an economic-base study into population or household terms by means of a normative conversion ratio, such as average number of dependents per worker. If available, income or output are equally acceptable as units of measure for an economic-base study and, for certain purposes, may even be preferable.

The next step is to identify the industries in the basic and service sectors. Then employment (or income or product) in each sector must be tabulated. Once this is done, the base ratio and base multiplier can be computed in the manner described earlier.

An economic-base study can serve regional analysis in many ways. Its findings can provide the basis for making estimates to fill gaps in historical data when only partial information is available, and they can assist in understanding past and current developments in the regional economy. The base multiplier is useful for evaluating or estimating the impact of an expanding or new industry in the region, particularly if the multiplier has been computed on an industry-by-industry basis. It can also serve as the foundation for estimates of future demand essential to the work of physical, public service, private enterprise, economic, and other planners and as the basis for estimates of basic jobs that must be created in order to reach target levels of total regional employment. Used only descriptively, the base ratio and base multiplier can provide valuable insights into the nature of the regional economy through interareal and intertemporal comparison.

OPERATIONAL CONSIDERATIONS FOR AN ECONOMIC-BASE STUDY

The first problem that confronts the regional analyst who sets out to perform an economic-base study is the selection of a unit of measure. The two most common units of measure employed in economic-base studies are employment and income.

As mentioned earlier, employment is generally the most available unit of measure, and it is easily converted into other terms, such as population and households. But using employment as the unit of measure poses some troublesome problems, such as the conversion of part-time and seasonal employment into equivalent full-time annual employment. There is also the problem of commutation.

Residents of the study region who work beyond its borders and residents of neighboring regions who daily commute to jobs in the region must be sorted out and accounted for appropriately. Furthermore, owing to technological, productivity, management, and related factors, employment may be a relatively insensitive measure of change, especially in the short run.

Income that accrues to residents of the region may in some cases be a more useful unit of measure, especially when the economic-base study is being used to gauge potential change in the region as a market. Some would argue that income also provides a more meaningful measure of changes in individual and community welfare than does employment. However, problems of data availability and reliability often preclude the use of income as a unit of measure in economic-base studies, especially in poor regions.

Sales and value added by enterprises in the region have also been used as units of measure for economic-base studies. Naturally, the value of the economic-base study is enhanced when performed using more than one unit of measure and the results based on the different units of measure are compared.

After a unit of measure has been selected, the analyst next must consider a method for determining which industries are in the basic sector and which are in the nonbasic sector. A direct method of sectoral determination, such as a survey in which firms and households in the region are asked to identify basic and service employment or income, would appear to yield the most precise information. Unfortunately, however, direct methods require a high quantity and quality of participation in the survey. Consequently, direct methods are often impracticable. Most analysts employ one of a variety of indirect methods of sectoral determination for economic-base studies.

The simplest indirect method is the assumptions approach, in which it is assumed that all of certain categories of economic activity are basic. A common assumption for economic-base analysis purposes is that all manufacturing and agricultural production is for export and that all remaining economic activity is supporting activity. In certain cases, especially as regards small and isolated communities, such assumptions are reasonable. In the majority of cases, however, many industries will be found to have significant components in both the basic and nonbasic sectors; and the economy will have an overall complexity that precludes such simplifying assumptions.

A second indirect method for estimating the proportions of economic activity that are basic and nonbasic, and one that seeks to identify the separate components within each industry, is based on the formula for the location quotient. The following formula derives directly from the formula for the location quotient given in Chapter 5:

$$X_r = \frac{\text{(National employment in industry x)(Total regional employment)}}{\text{Total national employment}}$$

The solution for X_r indicates the number of workers that would be employed in industry x in the region if regional employment in this industry relative to total regional employment reflected national employment in this industry relative to total national employment. The formula would, of course, work as well if income instead of employment were used as the unit of measure.

The location quotient method holds that the extent to which actual regional employment in industry x exceeds X_r represents regional specialization that is aimed at the export market and, therefore, is the part that constitutes basic employment in that industry. The total basic and service sectors can be computed by applying the location quotient formula to every industry represented in the region. For this purpose the regional economy could, of course, be divided up into as few as 2 or as many as 500 industries. The sum of the positive differences between actual and X_r values is the total for the basic sector, and all remaining employment is nonbasic.

Some analysts have employed variations of the location quotient method that tie the basic proportion of employment in an industry to the regional share of national population or income. Under this variation, if regional population or income is 5 percent of the national total, for example, then it is assumed that all employment or income in a regional industry in excess of 5 percent of national employment or income in that industry results from production for export and may therefore be counted as basic.

Methods based on the location quotient have come in for criticism; the general shortcomings of the location quotient are summarized in Chapter 5. Particularly serious when used in economic-base analysis is the failure of the location quotient to account for nonuniformity of demand and productivity throughout the country. Furthermore, the location quotient method ignores the fact that a certain proportion of national output is for foreign consumption.

In fact, the best approach in many cases will entail a combination of assumptions and location quotient. The output of certain specific regional industries can usually be taken as entirely basic, for all intents and purposes. Others can reasonably be taken as entirely nonbasic. The location quotient approach can be applied to those that probably are significantly active in both sectors. Or, a combination of direct and indirect methods of sectoral determination may be appropriate. Reasonable assumptions can be made about some industries; a location quotient technique can be applied to others; and a few key industries can be surveyed.

There is a host of problems concerning classification of industries, or parts of them, and the subsequent determination of the base ratio and base multiplier, that may be unique to certain regions or local areas. These problems often arise in connection with regions in which there is a large flow of workers who regularly cross regional borders, in which there are industries producing a wide variety of products for a wide variety of markets, in which a significant amount of economic activity is in industries whose products are not sold on the market, or in which other unique features prevail. In these situations the only way to classify industries correctly, apart from making rough estimates, is to conduct surveys that will supply the necessary information.

A further problem that the economic-base analyst will have to deal with is the time lag problem. One can readily appreciate that the base multiplier does not work instantaneously, that there is a time lag between the response of the basic sector to a change in exogenous demand and the response of the nonbasic sector to the change in the basic sector. The period of time required for the multiplier to work itself through is not known, and for most practical purposes it cannot be known.

A common approach to this problem is to ignore it, on the argument that over the long run whatever time lag may exist is of insubstantial consequence. Some analysts, especially when performing an economic-base study for projection rather than descriptive purposes, have tried to offset the problem through the way in which they calculate the base multiplier. Earlier, a formula for the base multiplier was given as follows:

$$\text{Base multiplier} = \frac{\text{Total employment}}{\text{Basic employment}}$$

However, some have suggested that the following will give better results, in view of the time lag problem:

$$\text{Base multiplier} = \frac{\text{Change in total employment}}{\text{Change in basic employment}}$$

Still other analysts have argued that if the base multiplier is to be used as a projection device, the time lag difficulty will best be offset through the computation of a historical time series of base multipliers in which the latter formula is used over a number of three-to-five-year periods. With the time series as a point of departure, an estimate of the value of the base multiplier at some point in the future becomes possible. A time series of base multipliers would also have descriptive analytical value with respect to the past development of the region.

A convincing projection of the base multiplier also would help overcome one of the major criticisms of projection-oriented economic-base studies, one that stems from the problem of the changing base ratio. In economic-base analysis, estimates of future impacts rest on present or past base ratios. However, successful development generally brings with it relatively radical structural change, particularly in the long run; and structural change inevitably expresses itself in a much-altered base ratio. Furthermore, one of the objectives of regional development is often an increase in the magnitude of the multiplier and a shortening of the time lag, whatever it may be.

The operational considerations of economic-base studies suggest that the effectiveness and usefulness of such a study increases, generally, directly with the degree of isolation and specialization of the study region, and inversely with its size. However, if executed carefully and used cautiously, an economic-base study can be a highly utilitarian tool for exploring, evaluating, and making rough estimates of trends in employment, income, population, housing needs, community services needs, and other aspects of the regional complex important to analysts and development planners. For an economic-base study to be relevant, it is necessary only that the economic-base theory seems a reasonable explanation for the growth of the region.

INCOME/EMPLOYMENT DETERMINATION

Economic-base analysis can be relatively simple and used for the kind of rough impact and trend assessment referred to so far. Or, it can be refined into a highly sophisticated, complex, and detailed tool for income, employment, or sales estimation and for guidance with respect to development policy for specific industries in the region or local area. Input-output analysis, discussed in Chapter 7 following, turns out to be a form of economic-base analysis taken to the limits of its possibilities. Between simple economic-base analysis and input-output analysis is a range of variants related to notions taken from income determination theory. For convenience, these will be explained in terms of income; but, as is often the case, they would apply in terms of employment and employment determination just as well.

In Chapter 1, a discussion that led eventually to the multiplier concept began with the basic components of product or income for a nation or subnational area: consumption spending, investment spending, government spending, and exports. For purposes of income determination, of concern are those portions of the four components that actually result in local income, as distinguished from the portions

that are leakages from the income-generating stream. Leakages
include spending on purchases outside the region, taxes, savings,
investments outside the region, and the like from which local residents and businesses do not derive current income. If these ideas
are merged with economic-base ideas, a two-step procedure suggests
itself: first, identify the components of the basic sector and, then,
determine the leakage proportions for each of them.

For purposes of income determination, the basic sector must
be thought of as encompassing those types of spending not directly
dependent on the current level of regional income or economic activity. It therefore includes not only exports, the spending for which
(or income from which) is obviously determined by demand exogenous
to the region, but also investment and government spending, or at
least large portions of them. Current levels of investment and government spending are determined substantially by decisions made in
the past, by expectations concerning the future, and by other considerations that are not related to current levels of local income or
economic activity, especially in the short run.

Income earned in the region is spent on regional consumption
and leakages. As luck would have it, not all regional consumption
expenditures (nonbasic sector spending) generate regional income.
Some pay for imports purchased through local agents or shopkeepers,
some pay for indirect taxes, and so on. A change in total regional
income, then, would be equal to the change in income or spending in
the region's basic sector times a multiplier. Basic sector income
results from purchases of the region's exports, regional investment,
and government spending in the region. The multiplier would be derived from the proportion of income spent on consumption in the region times the proportion of regional consumption spending that in
turn generates income in the region.

It will be recalled that the base multiplier formula is

$$\text{Base multiplier} = \frac{\text{Total income}}{\text{Basic income}}$$

Since total income = nonbasic income + basic income, the multiplier
formula could be written as

$$\text{Base multiplier} = \frac{\text{Total income}}{\text{Total income} - \text{Nonbasic income}}$$

If the right side of this last formula were multiplied through by total
income to reduce it to terms of one, the result would be

$$\text{Base multiplier} = \frac{1}{1 - \text{Nonbasic proportion of income}}$$

To digress for a moment, the nonbasic proportion of income is the proportion that generates further regional income. By definition, this is the proportion that does not leak out. So the multiplier formula could be written

$$\text{Base multiplier} = \frac{1}{\text{Leakage fraction}}$$

The reader should not be surprised to find that this is the same formula arrived at in Chapter 1, through different means.

It has been shown that nonbasic income results from nonbasic sector spending (regional consumption expenditures) times the proportion of that spending that generates regional income. And it has been shown that nonbasic sector spending is itself a proportion of total regional income. Hence, the multiplier formula in terms of 1 could be further detailed as follows:

Regional base multiplier

$$= \frac{1}{1 - (\text{Proportion of income spent in the regional nonbasic sector})(\text{Proportion that generates regional income})}$$

Now that the formula for the multiplier has been worked out, return to the beginning of the income determination discussion and see how the pieces fit together in an economic-base analysis framework. According to this framework we know that

Change in total regional income

= (Change in spending or income in the region's basic sector) (Regional base multiplier)

Using the components of the conventional income determination model one can say that

Change in income in the region's basic sector

= Change in export sales

+ Change in regional investment

+ Change in government spending in the region

If the formula for the multiplier is now recalled, the full economic-base income determination formula can be expressed as follows:

Change in total regional income

$$= \left(\begin{array}{l} \text{Sum of changes in spend-} \\ \text{ing on regional exports,} \\ \text{investments, and gov-} \\ \text{ernment activities} \end{array} \right) \left(\frac{1}{\begin{array}{l} 1 - \text{(Proportion of income} \\ \text{spent in the regional nonbasic} \\ \text{sector)(Proportion that gen-} \\ \text{erates regional income)} \end{array}} \right)$$

Suppose research based on sample surveys indicated that of each Mu. 1.00 of regional income, only Mu. 0.60 is spent on consumption in the region. And suppose it were also found that of every Mu. 1.00 spent on consumption in the region, only Mu. 0.50 became regional income, while the remaining Mu. 0.50 paid for goods imported for sale in the region. The value of the multiplier could be computed as follows:

$$\text{Regional base multiplier} = \frac{1}{1 - (.6)(.5)}$$

$$= \frac{1}{1 - .3}$$

$$= \frac{1}{.7}$$

$$= 1.43$$

In other words, the base ratio is 1:0.43, or for every additional Mu. 1.00 of income generated in the basic sector, Mu. 0.43 additional income will be generated in the nonbasic sector. Now, values for changes in regional income from exports, investment, or government spending can be estimated or hypothesized and multiplied by 1.43, yielding the change in total regional income. Or, the development planner may establish a target level of total regional income, estimate given components of the basic sector, and solve for the components that could be influenced.

One can readily see how this analytical structure could be expanded to any level of desired detail. Instead of taking regional consumption as nonbasic and all the rest as basic, a distinction could perhaps be made after all between investment and government spending that are fairly closely related to current regional levels of income and economic activity and those that are not. One could distinguish several different types of exports reflecting very different types of exogenous factors: agricultural exports, extractive exports, manufacturing exports, tourism, and so on. Useful distinctions could not only be made between local and central government spending, but between their operating and capital expenditures as well. Investment might be subdivided between housing and business investment as well as between investors from the region and foreign investors.

Yet a further refinement would be to recognize that some types of spending are basic in the short run but nonbasic in the long run. Tourism, for example, may be determined exogenously in the short run, but it can be dramatically influenced by economic developments inside the region over the long run. Investment, too, over the long run will be determined by economic developments inside the region. How long are the short and long runs? The short run is a period over which all types of spending, with the exception of those classified as regional consumption, may truly be considered exogenously determined. As for longer runs, they are defined by the selection of types of spending that are determined by factors outside the region and types of spending that are determined by what goes on inside the region.

The foregoing discussion of economic-base income determination was in terms of the change in total regional income. Obviously, the discussion could just as well have been in terms of income levels in a given year. If income data were available so that total income and income from the basic sector could be tabulated for a given year, the multiplier could be derived. From there, one could perhaps determine or estimate some multiplier components and derive others residually. This would allow the analyst to calculate rough indirect estimates of multiplier impacts for key types of spending.

CONSIDERATIONS FOR DEVELOPMENT PLANNING

Needless to say, an overriding consideration in designing an economic-base study is matching the data available with the objectives of the analysis. Both ought to be modest the first time around. As economic-base analysis becomes a regular part of the cyclic development planning process, the uses to which it is put and the data available for it can be expanded systematically.

Economic-base analysis at the regional level poses a dilemma. Is regional development planning best served by depth of analysis or breadth of analysis? A detailed income determination approach can yield a rich lode of information useful for development planning; but such detail is virtually impossible unless the region is taken in aggregate, as if it were spaceless. If a simple form of economic-base analysis is used, it can perhaps be applied to subregional areas, and an intraregional multiplier map can be developed showing how the effects of change are diffused throughout the region.

In working with economic-base analysis, one is implicitly accepting the underpinning economic-base theory. Is growth or decline of the regional economy in fact dependent solely on exogenous factors and the size of the multiplier? Perhaps only certain aspects of the economy of the region or local area function this way. Cannot some incomes rise, or effectively rise, because local residents produce more value in goods and services for each other? Care is needed to ensure that economic-base analysis is used in a way that is appropriate to the dynamics of the regional economy under study.

Finally, in using economic-base analysis to support regional development planning, one must be aware of the economic-base growth trap. From economic-base theory and analysis, it can clearly be seen that the rate of regional economic growth will increase as sales by the basic sector increase and as the multiplier increases. Development planners tend to leap from economic-base analysis to policies for increasing investment or export sales, on the one hand, and for increasing the multiplier, on the other. They forget that it is not merely growth linkages that basic-sector sales and larger multipliers offer, it is also economic dependencies. Basic-sector sales depend on factors totally exogenous to the region, so they are not really susceptible to regional development policy, at least not in the relatively near term. And a large multiplier means that a contraction in the basic sector will hit the nonbasic sector particularly hard.

The economic-base growth trap points to one of the major issues, perhaps the central issue, in planning for the economic development of a region or local area. The courses of action that maximize the rate of economic growth tend to be the same as those that maximize economic vulnerability. The region that grows the fastest is likely ultimately to suffer the sharpest decline. Conversely, a development policy that places high priority on diversification and relative regional self-sufficiency may be at the expense of a rate of current regional money income growth that is desperately needed. Good development planning seeks the balances between growth and stability that provide the optimum framework for development. At its best, economic-base analysis is used to help identify those balances.

EXERCISES FOR CHAPTER 6

1. One study claimed to have found that large, diversified, metropolitan areas, such as New York, tend to have multipliers of about 1.8, and that a multiplier of 1.3 has been derived for small, modestly diversified, metropolitan areas. It could be argued that an increase in the multiplier is an important goal of economic development, as it would seem to imply that more of the benefits of spending are passed on to the local population. Can the comparative level of the multiplier for a subnational region, therefore, be taken as one indicator of regional progress toward economic vigor? What would you expect the multiplier to be in a poor agricultural region? What might happen to the multiplier as agricultural incomes rise? What would the change indicate? What steps could be taken to improve a regional multiplier?

2. If you knew mothing more about a given region than that it had a very high base multiplier, what would you guess to be the situation with regard to its size and economic structure, assuming it is a growing region?

3. Suppose you are told that the region's high multiplier is based on employment, and you know that per capita income has barely increased over the past decade. What conclusions might you draw?

4. Given no other information, what might you speculate about the region in each of the following cases?

    a. The region has a high proportion of income spent in the regional nonbasic sector, but it has a low proportion of such spending that generates regional income.

    b. The region has a low proportion of income spent in the regional nonbasic sector, but it has a high proportion of such spending that generates regional income.

7

REGIONAL
INPUT-OUTPUT
ANALYSIS

The total product of the economy, by conventional accounting procedures, is the combined value of all the final products produced, or final sales, during a year. Total output, by input-output accounting procedures, is the combined value of all sales that take place, or total sales, during a year. The latter considerably exceeds the former because it includes interindustry sales of intermediate products sold as inputs to production processes. Final sales are made in response to final demand, or demand for final products. Interindustry sales come about in the course of satisfying input requirements to the production processes that ultimately lead to final sales.

An interindustry sale represents a flow of goods or services between intermediate industries, industries that purchase inputs for processing and further sale, expressed in money terms. While there may be a "seller" and a "purchaser" in the common commercial sense, an interindustry transaction may be considered to have taken place even if these are absent. A transfer of goods among factories under a single ownership may involve no direct payment, for example. Nevertheless, it is considered an interindustry sale, complete with a seller and a purchaser, in the input-output sense. The same principle applies to final sales; even a transfer to inventory is considered a final sale or delivery with reference to the current accounting year.

Input-output differs from other forms of social accounting, such as income and product accounting, in that it deals explicitly with interindustry transactions generated by the demand for final products. These transactions represent the "double counting" that is carefully avoided under other accounting systems. The input-output model provides a framework for arraying, processing, and analyzing data in order to enable an understanding of the interindustry structure of the economy and the implications of the unique structural interdependence that prevails. In fact, analysis based on the input-output model is often called interindustry analysis.

Input-output analysis divides the economy into two major components, suppliers and purchasers. Each of these has two subdivisions, in accordance with the scheme below. Suppliers include the following:

1. Intermediate suppliers: These purchase inputs to be processed into outputs, which they sell to other intermediate suppliers or to final purchasers.

2. Primary suppliers: These do not purchase inputs to make what they sell. What they sell is considered to be primary inputs to other industries. Payments to these suppliers of primary inputs do not generate further interindustry sales; they are final payments. Earnings of these suppliers essentially represent value added.

Purchasers include the following:

1. Intermediate purchasers: These buy the outputs of suppliers for use as inputs for further processing.

2. Final purchasers: These buy the outputs of suppliers in their final form and for final use. The level and composition of demand by final purchasers are determined exogenously (outside the system). Production to satisfy final demand generates intermediate purchases of inputs.

Intermediate suppliers and purchasers are one and the same industries. Their sales and purchases are related to each other, since their purchases of inputs are a function of the demand for their outputs.

Primary suppliers and final purchasers may or may not be one and the same. But in cases where they are the same (households, for example, both supply labor, a primary input, and purchase final-consumption goods), their activities as primary suppliers and as final users are taken as completely independent of each other.

THE THREE INPUT-OUTPUT TABLES

Input-output analysis employs three tables. The transactions table contains basic data concerning total flows of goods and services among suppliers·and purchasers during the study year. The flows are measured in (or converted to) money terms and are viewed as sales transactions between suppliers and purchasers.

The direct-requirements table, derived from the transactions table, shows the inputs required from suppliers by each intermediate purchaser per unit of output that it produces.

The total-requirements table, derived from the direct-requirements table, shows the total purchases of direct and indirect inputs
that are required throughout the economy per unit of output sold to
final purchases by any intermediate supplier.

Imagine an isolated island economy. There are no imports, no
exports, no government, no investment, no savings, no inventory.
Thus, everything is purchased, processed, sold, and consumed on the
island in the current period. There is only one final purchaser, households; there is only one primary supplier, also households. Households supply primary inputs such as labor and management. There
are only two processing industries, agriculture and a collection of
crafts industries that we will call manufacturing. Table 7.1 is the
transactions table compiled for the island economy based on reported
sales during the most recent accounting year.

The first row of data shows that of total sales of Mu. 100,000,
agriculture sold Mu. 10,000 of produce to itself for further processing
(seed, feed, fertilizers, and so on). It also sold Mu. 30,000 of produce
to manufacturing for further processing (industrial crops, foodstuffs
for canning, and so on); and Mu. 60,000 of agricultural sales were
sold to final purchases for home consumption. The first column of
data shows that in order to produce the Mu. 100,000 of total output,
agriculture had to purchase Mu. 10,000 in products from itself,
Mu. 5,000 in manufactured inputs, and Mu. 85,000 in primary inputs
(such as labor) from households. The manufacturing row and column
can be considered in a similar fashion.

The rows, then, show the distribution of each supplier's sales
to intermediate and final purchasers. The columns show the distribution of each purchaser's purchases from intermediate and primary
suppliers. Naturally, for any intermediate industry, total inputs will
equal total outputs. For the economy as a whole, total final purchases
will equal total primary inputs; this corresponds to the equality between product and income by conventional accounting procedures.
And of course, as the "southeast" figure of Table 7.1 shows, total inputs into the system will equal total outputs of the system.

The transactions table provides a rather complete view of the
interindustry flows of goods and services in the economy during the
study year. It does not, however, constitute a generalized analytical
tool. The question, then, is how to transform the basic transactions
data into a generalized statement of direct input requirements per
unit of output for each intermediate industry. The answer is, divide
the input figures in each intermediate-purchasers column by the number at the bottom of the column, total inputs for that industry.

Since total inputs equal total outputs, dividing each intermediate-
purchasers column through by the total will provide a distribution of
inputs per unit of output for each intermediate supplier. Table 7.2

TABLE 7.1

A Simple Input–Output Transactions Table
(in thousands of monetary units)

		Intermediate Purchasers		Final Purchasers (households)	Total Sales (outputs)
		Agriculture	Manufacturing		
Intermediate suppliers	Agriculture	10	30	60	100
	Manufacturing	5	10	35	50
Primary suppliers	Households	85	10	15	110
	Total purchases (inputs)	100	50	110	260

TABLE 7.2

A Simple Input–Output Direct–Requirements Table

Mu. 1.00 of Output By Requires Inputs From	Agriculture	Manufacturing
Agriculture	0.10	0.60
Manufacturing	0.05	0.20
Households	0.85	0.20
Total direct inputs	1.00	1.00

shows the results of this simple computation, arranged in the format
of a direct–requirements table. The final–purchasers column has
been dropped, because purchases by final purchasers do not represent
inputs for further processing. The direct–requirements table is often
called the table of technical coefficients, because it shows the technical production–function relationships between outputs and direct inputs.

The direct–requirements table provides the direct–requirements
coefficients necessary to calculate direct inputs required for any level
of demand for the output of any intermediate industry. If, for example, demand for agricultural products is expected to amount to
Mu. 50,000, Table 7.2 shows that satisfying this demand will require
direct intermediate inputs to agriculture of Mu. 5,000 in agricultural
products and Mu. 2,500 in manufactured products. Also, Mu. 42,500
in primary inputs (farm labor) will be required by agriculture from
households. The direct–inputs requirements were computed by multiplying each coefficient in the agriculture column by the expected
final demand of Mu. 50,000 for that industry's products.

In effect, every shopkeeper and farmer has a one–column direct–
requirements table for the business or farm, in mind if not on paper.
It is used to adjust orders for supplies in accordance with the output
planned for delivery. From the perspective of the firm, all sales are
final and all inputs are primary.

From the perspective of the regional or local economy, however, more than direct–input requirements must be considered in
analysis for planning. Direct inputs are only part of the total input
requirements of the economy; intermediate direct inputs must also be
produced, and their production will require additional inputs; these
are called indirect inputs. But then, where do the indirect inputs
come from? Producing them will require even more indirect inputs.

And so, there emerges a pattern of successive rounds, and the outputs of each round serves as inputs for the round that is one step closer to the final product.

The direct inputs can be thought of as the first round of input supplies. The first set of indirect inputs, those required to produce the direct inputs, can be thought of as the second round of input supplies. The next set of indirect inputs, those required to produce the second round, are the third round, and so on. Calculation of total input requirements from the direct-requirements table by the iterative method refers to computing all the rounds and summing the results.

To illustrate, let us imagine that our island was suddenly discovered by a party of explorers. They inform us that, as they have already sent back word of their discovery, we can expect a substantial influx of population during the coming year. Incredibly, the explorers have brought with them estimates of the increase in final demand that will result from the influx of population. When these are added to existing levels, it is calculated that sales of agricultural products to final purchasers will amount to Mu. 200,000 and that Mu. 100,000 of manufactured products will be purchased by final consumers, provided of course, that they are available.

The leaders of the island society are somewhat worried because they must plan to accommodate the expansion that will be required. To do this, they must know what the full impact of the higher level of final purchases would be upon each supplying industry. What is obviously needed is an input-output total-requirements computation.

Table 7.3 shows how total requirements might be computed from the direct-requirements table. If agricultural sales to final purchasers are Mu. 200,000, multiplying this number through the agriculture column of the direct-requirements table in Table 7.2 shows that direct inputs of Mu. 20,000 are required from agriculture, Mu. 10,000 are required from manufacturing, and Mu. 170,000 are required from the primary suppliers, households. This computation is shown in the second column of Table 7.3. Note that the first set of each pair of parentheses in the column contains the corresponding coefficient from the direct-requirements table. The second set of each pair contains sales for that industry from the previous column. In a similar fashion, the direct-input requirements to enable manufacturing to satisfy the anticipated Mu. 100,000 of sales to final purchases can be computed, as shown in the third column of Table 7.3. Total direct requirements necessary to satisfy the final demand for both agricultural and manufacturing products are shown in the fourth column of Table 7.3.

Total direct-inputs sales are then multiplied through their respective columns in the direct-requirements table in order to arrive at second-round inputs required (the first set of indirect inputs). The

TABLE 7.3

Illustrative Total-Requirements Computation from Direct-Requirements Table
(in thousands of monetary units)

	Sales to Final Purchasers	Sales as Direct Inputs			Sales as Indirect Inputs										
					Second Round			Third Round			Fourth Round				
		To Agr.	To Mfg.	Total	To Agr.	To Mfg.	Total	To Agr.	To Mfg.	Total	To Agr.	To Mfg.	Total	Total	Total Sales
By agriculture	200	(.1)(200) = 20	(.6)(100) = 60	80	(.1)(80) = 8.00	(.6)(30) = 8.00	26.00	(.1)(26) = 2.60	(.6)(10) = 6.00	8.60	(.1)(8.6) = 0.86	(.6)(3.3) = 1.98	2.84	37.44+	317+
By manufacturing	100	(.05)(200) = 10	(.2)(100) = 20	30	(.05)(80) = 4.00	(.2)(30) = 6.00	10.00	(.05)(26) = 1.30	(.2)(10) = 2.00	3.30	(.05)(8.6) = 0.43	(.2)(3.3) = 0.66	1.09	14.39+	144+
By households	—	(.85)(200) = 170	(.2)(100) = 20	190	(.85)(80) = 68.00	(.2)(30) = 6.00	74.00	(.85)(26) = 22.10	(.2)(10) = 2.00	24.10	(.85)(8.6) = 7.31	(.2)(3.3) = 0.66	7.97	106.07+	296+
Total				300			110.00			36.00			11.90	157.00+	757+
By all suppliers	300			300											

totals for the second round are, in turn, multiplied through the direct-requirements table in order to arrive at third-round inputs required. This procedure can continue endlessly, but Table 7.3 does not go beyond four iterations. After four rounds, the numbers are relatively small in this example, and it is a good guess that the error resulting from truncation will be minimal. Nevertheless, a plus sign has been added to the totals for indirect inputs in recognition of the fact that these totals represent slight underestimates.

The row at the bottom of Table 7.3 shows that in order to satisfy the anticipated Mu. 300,000 combined final sales of agricultural and manufacturing products, total sales of direct inputs of Mu. 300,000, and of indirect inputs amounting to over Mu. 157,000, will be required throughout the economy. The rightmost column of Table 7.3, total sales for each industry, shows that total sales of agricultural products alone will amount to over Mu. 317,000, total sales of manufacturing products will exceed Mu. 144,000, and sales of primary inputs by households will total over Mu. 296,000. This is the information that the island leadership needs in order to plan for the necessary expansion.

A word is in order concerning the role of primary suppliers (households) in the computation in Table 7.3. Because no inputs are required by primary suppliers, payments for primary inputs in any round are final payments that do not reappear in the next round. It will be noted in Table 7.3 that the combined total sales in each round is smaller than the combined total sales in the preceding round by the amount of sales by households in the preceding round, which can be thought of as a leakage from the interindustry stream.

It was mentioned earlier that ultimately total sales by primary suppliers must equal total final sales, just as income equals product by conventional accounting procedures. In Table 7.3, combined final sales amounted to Mu. 300,000, but through the iterative process, sales of primary inputs came to only Mu. 296,000+. This is accounted for by the fact that only four iterations were worked through. The more rounds computed, the closer the total primary inputs figure will come to total final sales. The limit of the iterative process would be reached and actual total sales for all industries attained when total sales by primary suppliers equaled total final sales. The gap between these two figures after a number of iterations provides an indication of the distance from actual totals.

The iterative method for computing total requirements seems to have worked well enough, and had we continued with it for several more rounds, even more precise results would have obtained. In the example of the island economy, all intermediate industries were aggregated into but two categories, agriculture and manufacturing. In most regions or local areas, however, the intermediate industries, for purposes of input–output analysis, will number between 10 and 50. It is easy to see that running through the iterations in order to compute total requirements can be a rather cumbersome procedure. This cumbersomeness can rise to prohibitive dimensions when total-requirements computations are needed for a large number of alternative levels and compositions of estimated final demand, or final sales. It would be useful to have a set of total-requirements coefficients that would enable "solving" readily for any estimated or hypothesized level of final purchases (final sales), just as there are direct-requirements coefficients for this purpose.

Furthermore, for purposes of descriptive analysis, a generalized statement of structural interdependence in the economy is needed. A set of total-requirements coefficients arranged in a tabular format would constitute such a statement, in the same way that the table of direct-requirements coefficients constitutes a generalized statement of direct technical relationships.

A total-requirements table can be computed from the direct-requirements table by applying the iterative method for Mu. 1. 00 in sales to final purchasers by each intermediate industry in turn. This has been done for agriculture in Table 7.4 and for manufacturing in Table 7.5. The figures in the rightmost column in each case show the total requirements from all components of the economy to supply Mu. 1. 00 of that industry's product to final purchasers. These two columns have been transferred to Table 7.6, the total-requirements table.

In Tables 7.4 and 7.5 it will be noticed that two sets of numbers are given for total sales by households. In parentheses are those that derive from the four iterations. But it is known that ultimately total sales by primary suppliers will equal final purchases; so if we set them equal to 1. 00, total indirect primary inputs can be calculated residually as the difference between final purchases (1. 00) and direct primary inputs (0. 85 for agriculture, and 0. 20 for manufacturing). This is shown by the two numbers not in parentheses, which are the numbers used in tabulating total requirements from all suppliers. It is not really necessary ever to compute the total-requirements coefficient for aggregate primary inputs, since it will always have a value of 1. 00 in each column of the total-requirements table. The point was made earlier that the gap between computed total primary inputs and final purchases provides an indication of the magnitude of the error arising from limiting the computations to only a few rounds. In this case the gap would be the amount by which computed total primary inputs is less than 1. 00.

The total-requirements table shows total sales by each industry per unit of output delivered to final purchasers by any intermediate industry. In Table 7.6, for example, it can be seen that for every

TABLE 7.4

Total-Requirements Computations: Agricultural Sales of Mu. 1.00 to Final Purchasers

| | Sales to Final Purchasers | Sales as Direct Inputs | | | Sales as Indirect Inputs | | | | | | | | | Total | Total Sales |
| | | | | | Second Round | | | Third Round | | | Fourth Round | | | | |
		To Agr.	To Mfg.	Total	To Agr.	To Mfg.	Total	To Agr.	To Mfg.	Total	To Agr.	To Mfg.	Total		
By agri-culture	1.00	(.1)(1.00) = 0.10	—	0.10	(.1)(.10) = 0.01	(.6)(.05) = 0.03	0.04	(.1)(.04) = 0.00	(.6)(.02) = 0.01	0.01	(.1)(.01) = 0.00	(.6)(.00) = 0.00	0.00	0.05	1.15
By manu-facturing	—	(.05)(1.00) = 0.05	—	0.05	(.05)(.10) = 0.01	(.2)(.05) = 0.01	0.02	(.05)(.04) = 0.00	(.2)(.02) = 0.00	0.00	(.05)(.01) = 0.00	(.2)(.00) = 0.00	0.00	0.02	0.07
By house-holds	—	(.85)(1.00) = 0.85	—	0.85	(.85)(.10) = 0.09	(.2)(.05) = 0.01	0.10	(.85)(.04) = 0.03	(.2)(.02) = 0.00	0.03	(.85)(.01) = 0.01	(.2)(.00) = 0.00	(0.14) 0.01	(0.14) 0.15	(0.99) 1.00
By all suppliers	1.00			1.00										0.22	2.22

104

TABLE 7.5

Total-Requirements Computations: Manufacturing Sales of Mu.1.00 to Final Purchasers

	Sales to Final Purchasers	Sales as Direct Inputs			Sales as Indirect Inputs									Total	Total Sales
					Second Round			Third Round			Fourth Round				
		To Agr.	To Mfg.	Total	To Agr.	To Mfg.	Total	To Agr.	To Mfg.	Total	To Agr.	To Mfg.	Total		
By agriculture	—	—	(.6)(1.00) = 0.60	0.60	(.1)(.60) = 0.06	(.3)(.20) = 0.12	0.18	(.1)(.18) = 0.02	(.6)(.07) = 0.04	0.06	(.1)(.06) = 0.01	(.6)(.02) = 0.01	0.02	0.26	0.86
By manufacturing	1.00	—	(.2)(1.00) = 0.20	0.20	(.05)(.60) = 0.03	(.2)(.20) = 0.04	0.07	(.05)(.18) = 0.01	(.2)(.07) = 0.01	0.02	(.05)(.06) = 0.00	(.2)(.02) = 0.00	0.00	0.09	1.29
By households	—	—	(.2)(1.00) = 0.20	0.20	(.85)(.60) = 0.51	(.2)(.20) = 0.04	0.55	(.85)(.18) = 0.15	(.2)(.07) = 0.01	0.16	(.85)(.06) = 0.05	(.2)(.02) = 0.00	0.05	(0.76) 0.80	(0.96) 1.00
By all suppliers	1.00			1.00										1.15	3.15

TABLE 7.6

A Simple Input-Output Total-Requirements Table

Every Unit of Delivery to Final Demand By — Requires Total Sales by	Agriculture	Manufacturing
Agriculture	1.15+	0.86+
Manufacturing	0.07+	1.29+
Households	1.00	1.00
Total requirements from all suppliers	2.22+	3.15+

Mu. 1.00 of output delivered to final purchasers by agriculture, total sales by agriculture to final purchasers, to itself, and to other intermediate industries (in this case, there is only one other) will be slightly more than Mu. 1.15. And total sales by manufacturing to all intermediate industries will be slightly more than Mu. 0.07. If primary sales are added in, total sales by all suppliers in the economy to all purchasers will be slightly more than Mu. 2.22 per Mu. 1.00 of output delivered to final purchasers by agriculture. Of the Mu. 2.22 total, Mu. 1.00 represents sales to final purchasers, Mu. 1.00 represents sales by primary suppliers, and Mu. 0.22 represents interindustry transactions. The manufacturing column of Table 7.6 can be explained in a similar fashion.

The reader may be struck by the similarity between the total-requirements coefficient and the economic-base multiplier discussed in Chapter 6. If the total-requirements coefficient for agriculture is 2.22, then for every Mu. 1.00 of exogenous demand that is satisfied by agriculture, a total of Mu. 2.22 in sales will have been generated. The economic base ratio can be thought of as 1.00:1.22 for agriculture. The interindustry base ratio can be thought of as 1.00:0.22, because for every Mu. 1.00 of final sales Mu. 0.22 of intermediate sales are generated. A multiplier of 2.22 may seem somewhat high, but we have been illustrating with a closed island economy without leakages.

Now, let us return once again to the final-demand estimate for the island economy. Armed with the total-requirements table, it would be unnecessary to compute total-input requirements by the iterative method as was done in Table 7.3. In effect, this has been done in advance through the computation of total-requirements coeffi-

TABLE 7.7

Illustrative Total-Requirements Computations Using the
Total-Requirements Table
(in thousands of monetary units)

Requires Total Sales by \ Final Delivery By	Agriculture	Manufacturing	Total
Agriculture	(200)(1. 15) = 230	(100)(0. 86) = 86	316
Manufacturing	(200)(0. 07) = 14	(100)(1. 29) = 129	143
Households	(200)(1. 00) = 200	(100)(1. 00) = 100	300
Total	(200)(2. 22) = 444	(100)(3. 15) = 315	759

cients. All that need be done now is to multiply the coefficients in each column of the total-requirements table by the corresponding final-purchases (sales) estimate.

Table 7.7 shows these computations for the island economy example. The column for agriculture in Table 7.7 shows total sales by each supplier required to satisfy the anticipated Mu. 200,000 of delivery to final purchasers by agriculture. The manufacturing column provides the same information for the anticipated Mu. 100,000 of delivery to final purchasers by manufacturing. The total column corresponds to the total sales column of Table 7.3 and shows total sales by each supplier for the combined Mu.300,000 of delivery to final purchasers.

The total for each column can easily be disaggregated into its final purchases, primary supplies, and interindustry sales components. Of the approximate Mu.759,000 of total output, for example, Mu.300,000 represents anticipated sales to final purchasers; Mu.300,000 represents sales of primary suppliers (income, or value added); and the remainder, Mu.159,000, represents total interindustry sales.

REGIONAL INPUT-OUTPUT ANALYSIS:
THE TRANSACTIONS TABLE

Figure 7.1 provides a sample format for a regional input-output transactions table. It is considerably more complex than the transactions of Table 7.1, because the regional perspective is interested in knowing the sources of final purchases and primary supplies and in distinguishing between regional or the local economy and the rest of the world.

Input and output summaries have been added to the transactions table at the right and at the bottom to provide a framework for recapitulation. Inside the double lines, the data matrix can be divided into four quadrants. The upper right is the final-purchases quadrant; this shows sales of commodities produced in the region by each regional intermediate supplier to each major category of final purchaser. The upper left is the interindustry quadrant, the heart of the input-output table, which shows interindustry sales by regional intermediate suppliers (listed at the left) to regional intermediate purchasers (listed at the top). The lower left is the final payments-primary inputs quadrant, which shows sales by primary suppliers to regional intermediate industries. The lower right is the final payments-final purchases quadrant, which records sales by primary suppliers directly to final purchasers. Some of the sales-by-imports rows to exports columns in this quadrant will have zero values because regional agents are not involved. The data for the transactions table represent total sales that have involved any element of the regional economy during the study year.

For purposes of regional analysis, intermediate suppliers and purchasers are those that are located in the region. Imported supplies, whether processed or not, are not intermediate inputs from the point of view of the regional economy because they do not require locally produced inputs for their production. Similarly, export sales, whether for intermediate or final uses, are not intermediate sales from the standpoint of the regional economy because they are not processed further within the region.

Unless the sources supplying the necessary sales data maintain exceptionally good records and are uniquely cooperative, the input-output analyst is likely to find that for many industries, total purchases will not equal total sales. It is common practice in such cases to add an additional row and column, both entitled "Undistributed." In these, residual discrepancies between the input and output totals are recorded; and the totals are thus brought into equality.

In input-output accounting, as in other forms of accounting, it is customary to attribute to wholesale and retail trade only the value of sales that represents gross margin, sales less cost of goods sold.

FIGURE 7.1

Regional Transactions Table Format

Purchasing Industries and Sectors

Regional Intermediate Purchasers

Supplying Industries and Sectors	Industry 1	Industry 2	...	Industry i	...	Industry n
Regional Intermediate Suppliers						
Industry 1	X_{11}	X_{12}	...	X_{1i}	...	X_{1n}
Industry 2	X_{21}	X_{22}	...	X_{2i}	...	X_{2n}
⋮						
Industry i	X_{i1}	X_{i2}	...	X_{ii}	...	X_{in}
⋮						
Industry n	X_{n1}	X_{n2}	...	X_{ni}	...	X_{nn}

Primary Suppliers (final payments):
- Households
- Gross business savings
- Government
- Labor
- Transfers to parent companies
- Central government
- Goods
- Others

Imports (Local)

Primary Suppliers

Summary:
- Total regional intermediate industries
- Total final payments
- Total purchases (inputs)

Input

Final Purchasers:

Export
- Net inventory change
- Central government
- Business

Local
- Households
- Government
- Investment
- Households

Output Summary:
- Total sales (outputs)
- Total final sales
- Total regional intermediate industries

109

If the value of goods sold were included in the sales figures for trade, other regional intermediate industries would show few, if any, sales to final purchasers. The bulk of sales to final purchasers would be registered in the trade industry because the larger part of the final sales of most industries reach final consumers, and many intermediate users as well, through wholesalers and retailers. Sales by suppliers are recorded in accordance with the purchaser for which they are destined, whether or not the trade industry plays a role. This practice does not alter the value of total output, and it may be violated in cases where it is important to trace flows precisely and to highlight trade linkages.

Final purchasers (final sales) includes all output destinations other than regional intermediate industries; therefore, it has both local and foreign components. Locally, in addition to households, sales for investment and sales to government represent final sales, and there may be others. Investment includes replacement as well as growth investment. Since it is not net of depreciation, it is often called gross investment or gross capital formation. Even though investment sales may be to regional intermediate industries, they are not considered intermediate sales because the goods purchased receive no further processing and are not resold. Export sales, in addition to those to households, include those to businesses (whether for investment or intermediate uses), those to the central government, and possibly others. Net inventory change also represents a final purchase with respect to the regional economy for the accounting year.

Customarily, wages, salaries, profits, property income, and other sources of personal income are considered final payments to households. In some cases, it may be desirable to disaggregate these by type of payment. In addition to households, local final payments include gross business savings (including capital-consumption allowances that either were made or ought to have been made to cover depreciation) and payments to government. All payments for goods and services imported to the region are considered final payments in the regional transactions table. Figure 7.1 provides examples of categories of imports that might be itemized.

The illustrative transactions-table format shown in Figure 7.1 is more detailed than may be necessary or feasible in the case of most poor regions or local areas. If only the interindustry quadrant is of real concern, the final-purchasers and primary-suppliers categories may be combined into a single column and row, respectively; or a distinction may be made only between local and foreign purchasers or suppliers.

The definition of industries, level of disaggregation, determination of exogenous and endogenous sectors, and the like must remain

FIGURE 7.2

Regional Direct–Requirements Table Format

		PURCHASERS					
		Industry 1	Industry 2	. . .	Industry i	. . .	Industry n
SUPPLIERS	Industry 1	X_{11}	X_{12}	. . .	X_{1i}	. . . . . .	X_{1n}
	Industry 2	X_{21}	X_{22}	. . .	X_{2i}	. . .	X_{2n}
	. . .	.	.	. . .	.	. . .	.
	Industry i	X_{i1}	X_{i2}	. . .	X_{ii}	. . .	X_{in}
	. . .	.	.	. . .	.	. . .	.
	Industry n	X_{n1}	X_{n2}	. . .	X_{ni}	. . .	X_{nn}
	Total regionally produced inputs						
	Total primary inputs						
Total direct inputs		1.00	1.00	. . .	1.00	. . .	1.00

matters for careful consideration in each individual case. Decisions regarding these matters will reflect unique regional characteristics; the analytical orientation of the input–output study; data availability; assumptions; and perhaps even social, cultural, and political factors. There are only two ironclad rules. First, the list of regional intermediate purchasers must be identical with the list of regional intermediate suppliers. And second, accounting procedures must distinguish in a meaningful way between regional intermediate industries and final-purchaser categories, on the one hand, and between regional intermediate industries and primary-supplier categories, on the other.

REGIONAL INPUT-OUTPUT ANALYSIS:
THE DIRECT-REQUIREMENTS TABLE

As can be seen in Figure 7.2, the regional direct-requirements-table format is essentially the same as that used in the island-economy example. As before, direct-requirements coefficients are computed by dividing through each regional intermediate-industry column of the transactions table by the column total. Final-purchaser columns do not appear because, by definition, their purchases are not for intermediate use from the standpoint of the region.

Frequently, primary-supplier (final-payments) categories are combined into a single primary-inputs row in the direct-requirements table, as has been done in Figure 7.2. However, in many cases, it will be desirable to retain primary-inputs disaggregation in order to observe the distribution among the various categories of final-payments leakages from the streams of regional interindustry purchases. This would not affect the way the direct-requirements coefficients are computed.

Each box in the direct-requirements table contains a coefficient that indicates the input required by the industry at the top from the industry at the left for each unit of output delivered by the industry at the top. Since each column must total to 1.00, there can appear no values in excess of 1.00. For any estimated or hypothesized output of any regional intermediate industry, direct-input requirements from all suppliers can be computed by multiplying each of the coefficients in the appropriate column by the total output figure.

REGIONAL INPUT-OUTPUT ANALYSIS:
THE TOTAL-REQUIREMENTS TABLE

The conventional total-requirements table format is essentially the same as the direct-requirements table format. In the case of the total-requirements table, each box in the data matrix shows total sales by the industry at the left when the industry at the top delivers one unit of output to final purchasers.

It is important to note that the coefficient appearing in any box does not indicate which industries purchased the input supplied by the industry at the left. The total-requirements coefficients include indirect inputs sold to all intermediate purchasers as well as direct inputs sold to the industry at the top of the column.

In the total-requirements table, all the boxes of the major diagonal of the data matrix, where each regional intermediate industry's row and column intersect, will have values greater than 1.00 (in some cases equal to 1.00, but never less than 1.00). This is because these coefficients reflect not only direct and indirect requirements but also the one unit of delivery to final purchasers. All other coefficients in any column will be smaller than the coefficient in the major diagonal. Apart from its conceptual significance, this characteristic of the total-requirements table can serve as an aid in spotting computational error.

In order to use the total-requirements table as a simulation-projection device, estimates of final sales must be given from elsewhere. All the coefficients in each column are multiplied by the given final-sales estimate for the industry at the top. Column totals will then show total outputs required from all regional intermediate industries in combination in order to enable satisfaction of the given final sales by the industry at the top. Row totals will show total output required from each of the suppliers at the left in order for the regional economy as a whole to satisfy the entire set of individual industry final-sales estimates.

We should now reconsider the method for solving the direct-requirements table for the total-requirements coefficients. Earlier, the iterative method was demonstrated with a set of hypothetical final-sales estimates. Then it was pointed out that if this procedure were followed on an industry-by-industry basis for a single unit of delivery to final purchasers (that is, final sales) by each industry, it would provide the total-requirements coefficients for the total-requirements table.

It was also noted that an indication of nearness to limit values of the iterative process is given by the nearness of total primary inputs to final purchases. But what is to be done once it has been determined that the iterative method has been worked out far enough? In the earlier examples, the iterations were simply stopped at this point, and the figures for each industry were summed for total requirements. This is not an entirely satisfactory procedure, however, and it leaves the analyst with the uncomfortable feeling that one more round would bring the computations one degree closer to actual values.

A procedure exists for estimating for each industry the total value encompassed by all the rounds that remain uncomputed after the cutoff point. There are five steps in the procedure, as follows:

Step 1: For each regional intermediate industry, compute the ratio of the increment in the last round to the increment in the next to the last round.

Step 2: Compute the average of these ratios among all the industries.

Step 3: Compute the ratio of this average to 1.00 minus this average.

Step 4: For each industry, multiply the increment in the last round by the ratio from step 3. This gives the approximation of the sum of the remaining uncomputed increments for each industry.

Step 5: Add these quantities to the totals for the corresponding regional intermediate industries.

While this rounding-off procedure enables greater precision, it also adds to the cumbersomeness of the iterative method. Clearly, when one works by hand or even with a desk calculator, the number of sectors that can be handled within reasonable limits of time and manpower using the iterative method is limited. At some point it becomes worthwhile to employ computers to do the job.

Once a computer is doing the computations, it is possible to obtain absolute accuracy through a mathematical method known as the matrix inverse method. Unless the interindustry matrix covers but a handful of regional intermediate industries, the matrix inverse method can be accomplished only by computer. The method entails performing a series of mechanical mathematical operations on the direct-requirements table, thereby converting it to a fully accurate total-requirements table. The coefficients that appear in the total-requirements table computed by the matrix inverse method represent the actual limits of the iterative process, limits that can never be fully attained through the iterative method. In fact, in much of the input-output literature, the total-requirements table is referred to as the matrix inverse table.

It is not necessary for the analyst to know the operations involved in the matrix inverse method. It is a standard mathematical procedure, and any computer will be able to use standard programs. All the analyst need do is supply the matrix of direct-requirements coefficients and request an $(I - A)^{-1}$ solution. In linear algebraic notation, this means the inverse of the matrix formed by subtracting the A matrix from the identity matrix. In this case, A is the matrix of direct-requirements coefficients. Table 7.8 is the total-requirements table for the island economy computed using the matrix inverse method and set up as if the island were a region. It should be compared with Table 7.6.

If disaggregation of primary inputs has been retained in the direct-requirements table, this disaggregation can be retained when employing the iterative method, so that the total-requirements table also shows primary-input detail. The matrix inverse method, however, handles only the square data matrix of the regional intermediate

TABLE 7.8

Total-Requirements Coefficients Derived by the
Matrix Inverse Method

Requires Total Sales By / Every Unit of Delivery to Final Purchasers By	Agriculture	Manufacturing
Agriculture	1.1594	0.8706
Manufacturing	0.0725	1.3043
Total regional intermediate inputs	1.2319	2.1749
Total primary inputs	1.0000	1.0000
Total requirements from all suppliers	2.2319	3.1749

industries. Thus, when the matrix inverse method is used, disaggregated primary inputs must be built back in after the total-requirements coefficients for regional intermediate industries have been computed.

In order to demonstrate how this can be done, we shall turn to the island-economy example for the last time. The interindustry matrix of the total-requirements table has been derived by the matrix

TABLE 7.9

Illustrative Direct-Requirements Table with Disaggregated
Primary Inputs

		Regional Intermediate Purchasers	
		Agriculture	Manufacturing
Regional intermediate suppliers	Agriculture	0.10	0.60
	Manufacturing	0.05	0.20
Primary inputs	Households	0.60	0.15
	Government	0.25	0.05
Total direct inputs		1.00	1.00

inverse method, and it appears in Table 7.8. However, the direct-requirements table of Table 7.9 will replace Table 7.2. The only difference between the two is that in Table 7.9 there are two primary-inputs categories, households and government.

If households and government were combined into a single primary-inputs row in the total-requirements table, the total-requirements coefficient appearing in every box of that row would be 1.00. It has been decided by the island's analyst, however, that households and government should each be represented by a row in the total-requirements table, so that their total-requirements coefficients can be considered separately.

Each of these coefficients can be computed as the sum of products resulting from multiplying each coefficient in the primary-inputs row of the direct-requirements table by the coefficient for the corresponding regional intermediate industry in the appropriate column of the total-requirements table. In effect, the direct-requirements primary-inputs row is turned sideways and aligned with the appropriate interindustry column, each pair of coefficients multiplied, and the products summed. Take, for example, the coefficient for households in the agriculture column of the total-requirements table. This would be the sum of products that resulted from multiplying the households row in Table 7.9 (0.60, 0.15) by the agriculture column in Table 7.8 (1.1594, 0.0725). Thus, (0.60)(1.1594) = 0.6956 and (0.15)(0.0725) = 0.0109; and the households total-requirements coefficient for agriculture is 0.6956 + 0.0109 = 0.7065.

The computations for the four primary-inputs total-requirements coefficients in the example are provided in Table 7.10. Table 7.11 shows how the results of these computations would appear in the total-requirements table with disaggregated primary inputs.

The reader with a background in linear algebra will recognize the procedure described as a matrix multiplication. This operation can also be handled by the computer. If disaggregated primary-inputs total-requirements coefficients are desired, the correct instruction to the computer operators would be as follows: multiply the matrix of primary-inputs direct-requirements coefficients (the premultiplier) by the $(I - A)^{-1}$ matrix (postmultiplier) and append the product matrix to the bottom of the $(I - A)^{-1}$ matrix. The computer printout will show the complete matrix of regional intermediate- and primary-inputs total-requirements coefficients. All that will remain to be done is to write in the names of the sectors at the left and top; and, of course, it can be arranged for the computer to do that as well.

TABLE 7.10

Computation of Total-Requirements Coefficients for Primary Inputs

| Primary Inputs Are Required By | When Delivery to Final Purchasers Is Made By | | | | | |
| | Agriculture | | | Manufacturing | | |
	Agriculture	Manufacturing	Total	Agriculture	Manufacturing	Total
And are supplied by						
Households	(.6)(1.1594) = .6956	(.15)(0.0725) = .0109	.7065	(.6)(0.8706) = .5224	(.15)(1.3043) = .1956	.7180
Government	(.25)(1.1594) = .2899	(.05)(0.0725) = .0036	.2935	(.25)(0.8706) = .2177	(.05)(1.3043) = .0652	.2829

117

TABLE 7.11

Illustrative Total-Requirements Table with Disaggregated
Primary Inputs

Requires Total Sales By	Every Unit of Delivery to Final Purchasers By	Agriculture	Manufacturing
Regional intermediate industries	Agriculture	1.1594	0.8706
	Manufacturing	0.0725	1.3043
Primary inputs	Households	0.7065	0.7180
	Government	0.2935	0.2829

INTERREGIONAL AND INTRAREGIONAL INPUT-OUTPUT STUDIES

Imagine a region that exports coal and simple metal products. One of its principal customers for coal is the country's single steel mill, located elsewhere. National projections show a rapidly increasing demand for metal products. An input-output model has been constructed for the region, and it shows that in order to satisfy the greater demand for its metal products, the region will require, among other things, substantially increased imports of steel inputs. However, the input-output tables do not show that as a consequence of the region's increased demand for steel imports, it will have to supply greater quantities of coal exports to the steel mill.

Or imagine a region with several small craft industries. The products of these industries, as well as many agricultural products, are marketed through a trading center outside the region. Projections show a growing regional population, and the regional input-output model indicates increased imports to satisfy the growth in final demand by local households. What the input-output tables do not show is that the increase in imports, purchased in large part directly or indirectly through the trading center outside the region, will result in a substantial increase in exports, because many of the imported goods originate in the region.

Interregional feedback effects like these can be introduced into the input-output analysis through an interregional input-output framework. In this framework, the list of intermediate industries is repeated at the top of the table to the right of the list for the study region and at the left of the table below the list for the study region, for each additional region covered by the interregional input-output study. For this purpose, the rest of the country may be considered a single "other region," or any number of other regions may be included. Thus, for any intermediate input that is imported to the study region, the transactions table will indicate the region and industry from which it was imported. Similarly, the destination region and industry for exports of the study region will be indicated. If only interregional transactions with the study region are to be considered, the table will be "dog-legged"; there will be no data matrices for transactions between the other regions exclusively.

In the absence of a full-fledged interregional input-output study, information on interregional linkages and feedback effects must be derived from a source beyond the framework of regional input-output analysis. Data from linkages, flows, and similar studies with an interregional orientation can provide the basis for final-sales estimates that will reflect the impact of interregional interdependence.

The analyst may find it useful to divide the region into subregions or subspaces when looking into its input-output structure. An intraregional framework can be set up to cover subregions in precisely the same manner as described for the interregional framework. It may be appropriate to divide the region into only two subspaces, the major urban center and the rest of the region. Or an intraregional framework may be set up to cover only selected industries.

CONSIDERATIONS IN PERFORMING AND
USING A REGIONAL INPUT-OUTPUT STUDY

Many of the operational considerations in performing an input-output study for a region or local area were covered earlier. There remain, however, a number of further problems that the analyst will have to deal with as appropriate in each individual case. Understandably, these problems increase with the complexity of the economy being studied; but then, so does the usefulness of input-output analysis.

The most obvious difficulty in using input-output tables is the problem of constant coefficients. In fact, technical-production coefficients are a function of the mix of specific products being produced, supply and market prices, the technology of production processes, the technology of materials inputs, external economies, input delivery times and reliabilities, binding contracts, traditional trade patterns, and more. The greater the industry detail in the tables and rate of innovation in the region, the less reliable will be the technical coefficients developed in the study for long-term analysis.

The fact that final payments are not always final and final demand is not always exogenous may also create a problem for the analyst. The most obvious example is labor. An increase in the demand for labor will result in increased incomes to households, which may, in turn, increase final demand and sales and therefore interindustry sales, even in the current period.

Several problems in input–output accounting are related to time concepts. Actual transactions during a single accounting year constitute the basis for the entire input–output structure. Any particular year may involve irregularities that bring the representativeness of the coefficients derived from the transactions data into question. Such irregularities may include major strikes, passing fads, unusually large inventories, and other temporary conditions.

Then there is the problem that stems from the fact that input purchases during one accounting year reflect not only requirements for current output. They also arise from anticipated output in the next accounting year, as well as inventory depletion that results from sales in the previous accounting year. This problem is reduced if inputs are counted to reflect consumption in the process of production rather than purchases by producers.

The regional input–output analyst is, of course, plagued with the usual problems of disclosure, data reliability, and the cost of data collection. Data problems are particularly acute in input–output analysis because of the level of detail that is required and the compounding of error in the process of deriving the total-requirements coefficients.

To all this may be added the problem of prices. Actual sales data may be found to be incomplete or unavailable. In such cases, estimation will require the pricing of physical output. This may be quite difficult, because most goods sell at one price for final purchasers and at another for intermediate purchasers. Producers' prices are usually preferred, but these may prove to be the most difficult to obtain or estimate. Furthermore, there is usually a gap between quoted and actual prices, in consequence of special agreements, bulk purchasing, and so on. Then, prices change during the year in accordance with seasonal variations, as the result of general inflation, or owing to other factors. The problem of pricing is a rather important one, not only because transactions data provide the basis for the technical coefficients, but also because they may provide the basis for conversion of findings of the input–output study into labor terms.

Many of these problems can be overcome by careful backup research and by analytical ingenuity. Some, however, are inherent in the input–output approach. This approach involves the assumption that each industry can be represented by a single linear homogeneous production function. This means, first, that each industry produces one product, and produces it uniquely and by a single production process. Second, input purchases by an industry are related only to, and change in direct proportion to, the level of current output of that industry. And third, there are no external economies or diseconomies, and therefore, the effect of simultaneous production by several different industries is equal to the sum of their separate effects.

Despite its shortcomings, there is a trend toward the increased use of input-output methods in regional analysis. Input-output analysis has been found to be a powerful and instructive tool. Also, it is an extremely flexible tool, adjustable to specific needs of many kinds, and compatible with and complementary to many other analytical methods.

In many cases, the chief value of input-output analysis may be its descriptive rather than its predictive capabilities, and these can be exploited to a significant degree even if the total-requirements table is not computed. As a descriptive tool, input-output tables present an enormous quantity of information in a concise and orderly fashion, provide a comprehensive interindustry picture, and point up the strategic importance of various industries and sectors. Input-output analysis can therefore highlight the true sources of regional economic change in a way not possible with any other method of analysis.

The process of compiling the transactions table, the major task in performing an input-output study, may itself yield unexpected benefits. This activity provides the development staff with a framework for tracing through the economic structure of the region in a systematic fashion. It also reveals data gaps and provides the opportunity for finding ways of overcoming them. And the data collected for the transactions table are useful for many other kinds of studies, regional income and product accounts being the most obvious among them.

The use of the input-output model as a projection device requires independent final-sales estimates. Hence, the reliability of the projections it produces will be at least as speculative as the final-sales estimates that are applied to it. Nevertheless, guessing the future is often an important part of the planning process, and the input-output model may provide the best available means for doing it.

Input-output analysis has perhaps been used most widely for selective simulation. This includes simulating the impacts of alternative levels of final sales in specific industries and simulating the impacts of changes in the regional economic structure that express themselves as altered technical coefficients.

Suppose it has been decided to expand a certain industry of the regional or local economy. The development planner must consider the adjustments necessary in order to accommodate this expansion and derive maximum benefit to the region from it. For example, What other industries will have to be expanded, and by how much? What other industries will gain through increased input availabilities?

What kinds of preparatory training will be needed in the various skills? What will be the full fiscal impact of the expansion? How will total employment, income, and demand be affected? What will be the full cost of the expansion to the region? Input-output analysis would provide whole or partial answers to the planning questions posed, or at least essential information needed to develop the answers. For any one industry, a special-purpose study could be performed instead, and at less cost than input-output analysis. But an input-output study will provide a reusable tool for testing a limitless number of scenarios.

SUPPLEMENTARY ANALYTICAL
TOOLS AND SHORTCUTS

Once the input-output transactions table is compiled, its immediate analytical value can be enhanced by reorganizing it into a triangulated format. Triangulation involves listing the regional intermediate industries by order of increasing structural interdependence.

The measure of structural interdependence, for purposes of triangulation, is the number of other industries to which each sells its output. A perfectly triangulated interindustry quadrant of the transactions table would appear similar to that in Figure 7.3, in which each X represents interindustry sales and a blank represents a zero value. Triangulation will never produce the perfectly symmetrical pattern shown in Figure 7.3, but it should produce a pattern that tends in that direction. The triangulated order of industries, listed from top to bottom in accordance with increasing structural interdependence, should conform approximately to the order of industries when ranked in accordance with final sales as a decreasing proportion of total sales.

Triangulation provides immediate insights into the role of each industry in the regional network and into the hierarchical nature of the regional interindustry structure. These insights are of major analytical value and carry over into subsequent phases of the input-output study.

Many input-output analysts have found it helpful to assemble a destination-of-output table. For each industry, including primary suppliers, the percentages of total output sold to regional intermediate purchasers as a group and to final purchasers as a group are computed on the basis of data in the transactions table. Industries are then listed in the destination-of-output table in rank order by descending percentages of their total output sold to regional intermediate industries.

From the input-output direct-requirements table, a sources-of-inputs table can be assembled. For each regional intermediate-

FIGURE 7.3

Triangulated Interindustry Quadrant, Transactions Table

		Regional Intermediate Purchasers												Final Purchasers
		Retail trade	Construction	Hotels and tourism	Personal services	Fisheries	Quarries	Agriculture	Wholesale trade	Food products	Real estate	Crafts	Utilities and transport	
Regional Intermediate Suppliers	Retail trade	X												
	Construction	X	X											
	Hotels and tourism	X	X	X										
	Personal services	X	X	X	X									
	Fisheries	X	X	X	X	X								
	Quarries	X	X	X	X	X	X							
	Agriculture	X	X	X	X	X	X	X						
	Wholesale trade	X	X	X	X	X	X	X	X					
	Food products	X	X	X	X	X	X	X	X	X				
	Real estate	X	X	X	X	X	X	X	X	X	X			
	Crafts	X	X	X	X	X	X	X	X	X	X	X		
	Utilities and transport	X	X	X	X	X	X	X	X	X	X	X	X	
Primary Suppliers														

industry column, coefficients that represent regional intermediate inputs are summed. Industries are then listed in the sources-of-inputs table in rank order by descending percent of their total inputs from regional intermediate suppliers.

The major task in performing an input–output study is the collection of the relatively large quantity of transactions data. Because capabilities for accomplishing this are often limited, one of a number of partial input–output techniques may be preferable to the full-scale study.

One frequently used shortcut is known as the rows-only method. It is often possible to obtain data for total shipments or sales of a regional industry, but not distribution among purchasers. If this is the case, the analyst might attempt to distribute total sales among the purchasing industries on the basis of information obtained from a selected sample of supplying enterprises. The surveyed enterprises need only be asked to provide information on the percentage distribution of shipments or sales among purchasing industries. Firms will generally be more cooperative in supplying information when money values are not requested.

Following this procedure on an industry-by-industry basis provides the distribution among purchasers of the output for each row. Of course, when all the rows are filled in, the columns will also be filled in. The disadvantages in this method are that the distribution of sales is based on an indirect estimating procedure, and the benefit of a crosscheck by an independent determination of input data is lost.

Another partial input-output technique that drastically reduces data requirements is the major-minor method. Figure 7.4 conveys the principal idea. Regional intermediate industries are divided into groups of major ones and minor ones. Major industries are listed to the left and top, and minor industries are listed to the right and bottom along the interindustry quadrant. This has the effect of subdividing the quadrant into four subquadrants. The Xs in the data matrix of Figure 7.4 represent transactions involving a major industry. These are the only boxes in the interindustry matrix for which complete data are collected.

The remaining boxes represent transactions between minor industries and minor industries. Each column and row within this submatrix is handled as if it were a single box. In other words, a single sales value is derived for each (⇔), and it is not distributed among the columns encompassed. Similarly, a single undistributed purchases total is derived for each ⇕. Thus, time and expense are reduced by minimizing detail where transactions among minor industries exclusively are concerned. If necessary, the major-minor method can be taken to the extreme, in which minor industries are represented by a single row and a single column.

These supplementary analytical tools and shortcuts are but a suggestion of the possibilities for variations on the input-output theme. The input-output framework really is quite flexible. In designing an input-output study to serve the planning process for a region or local area, the opportunities for simplifying, modifying, and selectively applying input-output will be many. They arise from known features of the structure of the local economy or limited objectives for the study, and they should be fully exploited. It is not that regional data

FIGURE 7.4

Major–Minor Method, Interindustry Quadrant, Transactions Table

| | | | Regional Intermediate Purchasers | | Final Purchasers |
| | | | Major Industries | Minor Industries | |
			Industry 1 / Industry 2 / Industry 3 / Industry 4	Industry 5 / Industry 6 / Industry 7 / Industry 8 / Industry 9 / Industry 10	
Regional Intermediate Suppliers	Major Industries	Industry 1	X X X X	X X X X X X	
		Industry 2	X X X X	X X X X X X	
		Industry 3	X X X X	X X X X X X	
		Industry 4	X X X X	X X X X X X	
	Minor Industries	Industry 5	X X X X		
		Industry 6	X X X X		
		Industry 7	X X X X		
		Industry 8	X X X X		
		Industry 9	X X X X		
		Industry 10	X X X X		
Primary Suppliers					

are used to run an input–output study; it is, rather, that an input–output study is used to provide needed regional data.

Further discussion on the use of input–output analysis in a regional-planning context will be found in Chapter 8.

EXERCISES FOR CHAPTER 7

1. Given the following sales data (in thousands of monetary units) for a region in a particular year, complete the three input-output tables. Carry calculations through two rounds of indirect inputs, or a total of three rounds, and truncate. Round off calculations to three places right of the decimal point.

	Total Sales	Sales to Regional Processing Sectors		
		Agriculture	Manufacturing	Services
Agriculture	2,500	500	1,130	100
Manufacturing	1,500	20	120	40
Services	1,000	10	150	90

2. Provide a brief interpretive analysis and suggest planning implications based on the results of exercise 1.

3. In exercise 1, what will be the impact if final demand for agricultural products doubles?

4. What will happen to the interindustry structure of exercise 1 if technology in regional manufacturing changes such that double the present proportion of inputs from itself are required at the expense of agriculture's proportion of inputs to manufacturing?

PART III

THE PLANNING CONTEXT

8

SOCIAL ACCOUNTS
AS AN ANALYTICAL
FRAMEWORK FOR
DEVELOPMENT PLANNING

The term <u>social accounts</u> refers to the various accounting-based methods of analyzing the economy. They are social in that their focus is the economy of the national, regional, or local society rather than an economic enterprise. They are accounts in that they are based on the double-entry principle that every transaction is an exchange and can be represented as two flows of equal value in opposite directions. In Chapter 3 the best-known of the social accounts, income-and-product accounts, was introduced. In Chapter 4, balance-of-payments statements were discussed. In Chapter 7 input-output analysis was explained. Each of these is a form of social accounting; in each case the total of flows in one direction equals the total of flows in the other direction.

The thought may already have occurred to the reader that there must be some way to combine the three social accounts into a single system that provides a multifaceted overview of the region. The underpinning logic of the social accounts suggests linkages among them. Input-output analysis focuses on interindustry relationships, but final payments and final purchases are roughly equivalent to income and product. One of the components of gross regional product (GRP) is net exports, or exports minus imports. It is largely these exports and imports that give rise to the financial inflows and outflows on which balance-of-payments statements focus. One can also think in terms of input-output analysis concerning itself with what goes on among the industries of the regional economy, income-and-product accounts going on from there to examine the effect of these interactions on the region in aggregate, and balance-of-payments statements taking us one step further to look at what all this means in terms of the values of flows across the borders of the region or local area.

The three types of social accounts can in fact be combined into a single composite social accounting matrix. However, this involves some rearrangement of the accounts, and an approach to income-and-product accounting and balance-of-payments accounting that is at variance with the straightforward flexible approaches set out in earlier chapters. Moreover, in the vast majority of cases, social accounting at the level of the region or local area is likely to be rudimentary and indicative at best, and it hardly makes sense to design an elaborate composite matrix with a complex set of guiding assumptions and procedures for purposes of manipulating sketchy and relatively aggregate data. Better, for the practical purposes addressed by this book, to think of the social accounting system as a sequence of the three types of accounts rather than as a wholly unified framework that incorporates them simultaneously. Each of the three types of accounts can help with estimating and cross-checking data for the other two. Each can provide analytical insights complementary to those derived from the other two. Taken together they can be a practical guide to data collection and other types of analysis needed, as well as a conceptual guide to thinking about interrelationships, analysis, and development planning for a region or local area.

RUDIMENTARY SOCIAL ACCOUNTS

A development planning effort has just been launched in Region R. The initial-analysis framework that will provide information for it is modest, experimental, and has been designed with the knowledge that the data assembled at the outset will not be highly refined. One of the purposes of the initial-analysis framework is to uncover critical data gaps and provide a base of experience for the learning process that will lead over time to a finely tuned information system carefully coordinated with an ongoing planning process. A basic statistical compendium has been completed, and now some of the data it contains are being systematically analyzed with the help of several methods of regional economic analysis, including rudimentary forms of the social accounts.

Table 8.1 shows Region R's input-output transactions table compiled for the year 19XX. Direct-requirements coefficients have been added in the parentheses. From this table it can be seen that only in the case of manufacturing would moderate changes in annual output have significant interindustry implications. It can also be seen that only a third of regional manufacturing production is sold outside the region; that agriculture provides the major regional interindustry input to manufacturing; and that services, the smallest of the regional intermediate industries, provides a disproportionately large share of regional inputs to manufacturing.

From a development perspective, strengthening regional manufacturing exports would appear to be an effective means of ex-

TABLE 8.1

Input-Output Transactions Table with Direct-Requirements Coefficients, Region R, 19XX

(millions of monetary units; direct-requirements coefficients in parentheses)

| | Regional Intermediate Purchasers | | | | | Final Purchases | | Total Sales |
	Agriculture		Manufacturing		Services		Regional	Export	(outputs)
Regional intermediate supplies									
Agriculture	15	(.03)	30	(.12)	10	(.05)	145	250	450
Manufacturing	5	(.01)	20	(.08)	5	(.03)	135	85	250
Services	10	(.02)	20	(.08)	5	(.03)	105	60	200
Primary supplies									
Regional	370	(.82)	100	(.40)	135	(.68)	45	20	670
Import	50	(.11)	80	(.32)	45	(.22)	100		275
Total purchases (inputs)	450	(1.00)	250	(1.00)	200	(1.00)	530	415	1,845

panding the markets for regional agriculture and services. This might require greater production efficiencies to improve the competitiveness of regional manufacturing, a move that unfortunately is likely to reduce the already small proportion of local labor inputs to this industry even more. However, agriculture and services purchase over 80 percent and 65 percent, respectively, of their inputs from local primary suppliers, so expanding manufacturing exports will probably expand regional employment a good bit. In fact, the availability of additional workers in regional agriculture and services is probably essential for the expansion of regional manufacturing. Regional manufacturing already imports about a third of its inputs, and if regional benefits from an expansion in manufacturing activity are to be maximized, care must be taken to assure the availability of all inputs that could possibly be supplied locally.

If similar analyses were made for each of the other regional intermediate industries, a package of interrelated regional-development policies and activities could be derived. Such a package might include direct actions that should be undertaken, such as modernizing the manufacturing industry; measures needed to provide indirect support in the interest of maximizing regional benefits from those actions, such as training more workers for agriculture and the services industry; additional methods of analysis that could provide further insights, such as mix-and-share analysis; and additional studies that should be undertaken, such as one to identify the imported inputs to manufacturing for which local inputs might be substituted. Of course, Region R planners would not commit energy and scarce development resources to specific policies and activities without first considering information in the other social accounts.

Looking back at Figure 3.2 in Chapter 3 it can be seen that the basic idea behind income-and-product accounts is that the sum of expenditures (or sales) measures gross regional product on the right side of the accounts, while the left side of the accounts reflects the distribution of costs incurred in producing the product. How is it that among the expenditures those by businesses other than for investment are not found, and among the costs incurred in producing the product the costs of intermediate inputs are not found? The answer is, the income-and-product accounts count only final purchases and final payments. The logic of this becomes clear when it is recalled that in developing the input-output total-requirements table, the full value of final purchases ultimately ends up, when all the rounds have been worked through, in final payments for primary inputs. The income-and-product accounts, then, provide a picture of the aggregate regional final implications of interindustry relationships as a consequence of the response of the regional economy to final demand.

Figure 8.1 shows the income-and-product accounts designed and compiled by Region R analysts for 19XX. It is somewhat ambitious for a first effort, but the fact that a number of major enterprises are government owned makes certain information available that otherwise would be difficult to obtain; and this in turn facilitates estimates of other information based on residuals. Owing to the particular character of Region R and the data available, regional personal-consumption expenditures and investment in housing have been combined. The analysts have separated investment data for private and government enterprises because the decision making for them comes about in different ways and because the central government owns all government enterprises, while most private enterprises, including farms, are owned locally. Separate figures have been estimated for growth, replacement, and inventory change because each of these types of investment has different implications for regional development. For the same reason, separate estimates have been made for government capital construction and for operations expenditures.

The first few rows of the accounts shown on the left side of Figure 3.2 are encompassed by "regional personal income" on the left side of Figure 8.1. Personal income represents payments to factors of production—land, labor, and capital. But, of course, people own the factors of production, so such payments are really personal income. The other items on the left side of Figure 8.1 represent other costs of regional production, the payments for which do not accrue as income to residents of the region. Statistical discrepancies have been distributed proportionally among components of the accounts.

Figure 8.1 raises some questions and highlights some areas of potential concern with regard to Region R, though the accounts would be much more instructive if they were available for several years so that comparisons over time could be made. About 45 percent of regional product does not end up as income to residents of the region. Business transfers to nonresident owners amount to 30 percent of GRP, and business taxes seem close to insignificant. While Mu.67 million is estimated to be the amount of capital used up in producing the GRP, the right side of the accounts shows that only Mu.11 million is estimated as having been spent for replacement; and, although this may not be cause for alarm in any one year, the relationship between these figures should be watched carefully over time. Government has spent nothing to expand the productive capacity of its enterprises in the region in 19XX, while the private sector has spent Mu.25 million. Why? Does the fact that inventories of government enterprises grew by Mu.10 million while those of the larger private sector grew by only Mu.7 million offer a clue? Replacement investment in government enterprises seems rather low. Is there a suggestion here of inefficient enterprises building up unsold inventory while plant and equipment deteriorate, a situation that could lead to collapse and unemployment in the near future?

FIGURE 8.1

Income–and–Product Accounts, Region R, 19XX

(in millions of monetary units)

Regional Income and Other Charges against Gross Regional Product		Gross Regional Product			
Regional personal income	369	Regional personal–consumption and housing expenditures			376
		Regional business investment			53
		Private		41	
		Growth	25		
		Replacement	9		
		Inventory	7		
Business transfers	201	Government		12	
		Growth	0		
		Replacement	2		
		Inventory	10		
Business taxes	33	Regional government nonbusiness expenditures			101
		Capital construction	10		
		Operations	91		
		Net exports			140
		Exports	415		
Capital consumption	67	Imports	275		
Gross regional product	670	Gross regional product			670

TABLE 8.2

Balance-of-Payments Statement, Region R, 19XX
(millions of monetary units)

Item	Exports and Payments Inflows (+)	Imports and Payments Outflows (−)	Net
Current account			
Business sector			
Agriculture	250		
Manufacturing	85		
Services	60		
Transfers		201	
Total	395	201	+194
Government sector (nonbusiness)			
Tax revenues		33	
Capital construction	10		
Operations	91		
Total	101	33	+68
Consumer sector and unspecified	20	275	−255
Residual capital and cash movements			+7

While all this is somewhat sketchy, the potential implications for the development strategy suggested by Table 8.1 are clearly major.

From the data available, Region R analysts constructed the rudimentary balance-of-payments statement for 19XX shown in Table 8.2. Only current account information was available, so capital and cash movements were estimated residually. Exports by regional industries were taken from Table 8.1, as were consumer and unspecified exports and imports. Business transfers and government nonbusiness data were taken from the income-and-product accounts of Figure 8.1.

The balance-of-payments statement seems to open up a new perspective on the economy of Region R. Looking at the balance of payments rather than just exports and imports of goods and services raises new questions and concerns. It turns out that over 50 percent of the gains from export sales by Region R are wiped out by transfer payments to nonresident owners. It is known that the majority of transfer payments are from government enterprises in Region R to the central government treasury. This represents not only a direct loss of regional income but, through the multiplier, the loss in terms of regional welfare is compounded. Tax revenues paid to the central government are only through business taxes on the operations of private enterprises, which probably accounts for why they are so low; the central government spends an amount over three times this figure on capital construction and operations in the region.

Despite the fact that exports from Region R amount to nearly 60 percent of GRP, the balance of payments approaches the break-even point. In fact, the economy of Region R, which is relatively poor, subsidizes the rest of the country relatively heavily. The balance-of-payments statement brings further into question the viability of the manufacturing-export promotion strategy suggested by Table 8.1. It now appears that progress in regional development will require not only modernization, particularly in manufacturing, and a reduction of dependence on imports, but it may require as well a restructuring of effective ownership patterns or of modes of central-government operation in the region.

The reader is encouraged to extend the Region R exercise by expanding the interpretive analysis of the tables and figure in this chapter and identifying additional implicit linkages among them.

IMPROVING THE SOCIAL ACCOUNTS
AS AN ANALYTICAL FRAMEWORK
FOR DEVELOPMENT PLANNING

We will not here be able to delve more deeply into the problems of Region R or into potential development strategies for the area. There is obviously a complex of interrelated political, administrative, social, technological, and economic circumstances to be accounted for. We do, however, want to consider relatively modest steps the analysts for Region R might take to improve the system of social accounts for purposes of analysis for development planning. The improvements possible are of four related types: increased detail, strengthened linkages among the accounts, sharpened focus, and development of time-series data.

There are many ways the amount of detail in the accounts can be increased. Factors to be considered include: sectors, industries, or issues of special concern regarding which increased detail would provide decidedly improved insights; the types of additional data that can readily be obtained; key bits of information that enable further estimates through residual calculations or other means; and types of information that can serve a variety of analytical purposes.

For example, in the case of Region R, two types of detail readily stand out as highly desirable: disaggregated regional final payments and disaggregated imports. The former would permit more refined analysis of the actual regional benefits of the expansion in any industry, and the latter would enable planners to begin to consider local inputs that could be substituted for imported inputs. The income-and-product accounts of Figure 8.1 suggested that a portion of the regional final payments in Table 8.1 were not ultimately regional at all, and the balance-of-payments statement in Table 8.2 confirmed this. The larger portions of regional final payments and imports are generated in the agricultural, manufacturing, and services industries, as Table 8.1 shows. This means that most of the desired detail can be obtained through the same sample surveys and other techniques used to obtain the interindustry data for the transactions table (most enterprises are more readily able and willing to identify sources of inputs than ultimate destinations of output). It also means that the remaining portions of regional final payments and imports can be estimated roughly or not at all without diminishing the value of the analysis; refinement of those portions is less urgent and can await future efforts.

If regional final payments are detailed according to the components of "regional income and other charges against GRP" of the income-and-product accounts, then the data will also enable a partial disaggregation by regional industry of origin of the left side of those accounts. And if imports are detailed according to whether they are agricultural, manufacturing, or services imports, that information will enable a partial further disaggregation of the balance-of-payments statement.

Thus, if next year Region R analysts increased detail in the social accounts in the manner described, they not only will have done so with minimal additional effort, they at once will have generated greatly expanded insights regarding major planning issues, strengthened the linkages among social accounts and produced data useful for all of them, and sharpened the focus of the accounts. Furthermore, by building on the initial set of accounts rather than introducing wholesale revisions, consistent time-series data can be built up, further enhancing the usefulness of the social accounts over time. (The reader may find it instructive to introduce the improvements suggested in the transactions table, fabricating the data, and carrying the changes through all three social accounts.)

Of course, Region R analysts may have improved the accounts in other ways as well. They may have chosen to expand detail considerably more, but only for regional manufacturing or government enterprises or some other industry or sector of special concern. They may have chosen to augment the social accounts with other methods of analysis rather than modify the accounts themselves. They may have chosen to undertake special studies to uncover specific information not adequately encompassed by the methods of regional economic analysis. Or they may have selected a combination of these.

9

LIMITED
APPROACHES TO
ANALYSIS AND
PLANNING

The luxuries of an extensive information system, a framework of all the desirable methods of analysis, and a fully elaborated planning process are not always available to the development practitioner. These things require time and resources. As an appreciation for the potential benefits of development planning has spread, a demand has grown for limited approaches to analysis and planning. The need is for approaches that lead to a rapid identification of development projects and project priorities within at least a minimal long-term, strategic, economic development framework.

In response, this subject has been receiving increasing attention. Discussions may now be found in the literature concerning the Themes-Strategies-Project (TSP) approach, the Sketch-Planning approach, Reduced Planning, Environmental Planning and Management (EPM is a system that uses the environment as a focal point for integrating development activity), and other approaches designed to produce quick results. All of these approaches have in common ease and speed of application while laying the foundation for a more elaborate structure of analysis and planning that can be introduced in stages over time. The subject is treated at some length in Action-Oriented Approaches to Regional Development Planning, edited by the present author with Peter P. Waller and published by Praeger Special Studies in 1975. The material in that book and in other publications listed in the Bibliography (which can be readily identified by their titles) will not be repeated here.

This chapter introduces some notions that will be helpful to practitioners who need to design their own limited approaches to analysis and planning. Two subjects are discussed briefly: limited approaches to overall planning, and limited planning approaches based on project evaluation. The aim of the discussion is to convey ways of dealing with the problem that have proved themselves in practice. As with the discussions of methods of analysis, it will remain for the reader to elaborate on the principles suggested and develop a limited approach to analysis and planning uniquely suited to the circumstances of the region or local area at hand.

LIMITED APPROACHES TO OVERALL PLANNING

"Limited approaches to overall planning" refers to developing a strategic framework for economic development activity that will lead to identifying desirable projects, but in a manner that does not encompass all the steps or have the scope that might be desirable in a full-fledged development-planning process. They can be used as building blocks for expanding the structure gradually, so that over time the desirable steps and scope will be achieved. A reasonable alternative to not planning is planning a little bit. Most often planning begins when resources are few, time is short, and the need pressing. Without overall planning, however limited, the region or local area is likely to be denied the full benefit of projects undertaken. And of course, there are many stories of projects undertaken without a broad strategic framework that did more harm than good. The question often is, how do you best plan a little bit?

The answer is, concentrate on the principal concerns and limit analysis to that needed in order to address the principal concerns.

Regional economic development planning can be thought of as planning in several dimensions: economic activity, geography, time, and levels of organizational administration from the individual enterprise to the national government. If we think of economic activity in terms of sectors, and if we think of geography and levels of organizational administration as facets of regional space, we can use the convenient terminology associated with the EPM system mentioned earlier: regional economic development analysis and planning is concerned with coordination among sectors, space, and time. This provides a convenient basis for identifying initial principal concerns upon which to focus first planning efforts.

Figure 9.1 suggests one way of thinking about these three dimensions in a regional analysis and planning context. No dimension really exists on its own; one can visualize the region as an infinite number of intersections of the three dimensions. Some of those intersections are of greater immediate concern than others. Those are the ones upon which the planning process and supporting economic analysis should concentrate initially.

To some this may seem excessively structured; and indeed, the idea is to impose structure upon the decisions concerning how to

FIGURE 9.1

Regional Analysis and Planning: Sectors, Space, and Time

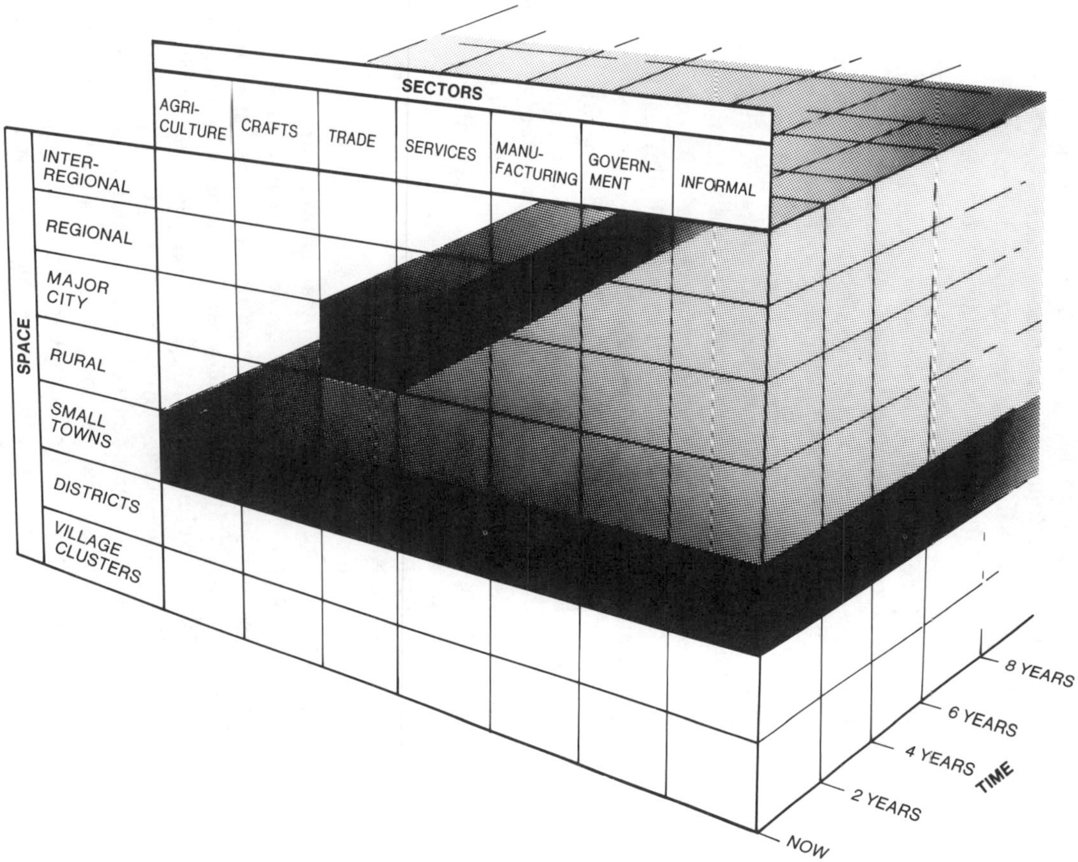

limit the planning process. In the absence of such structure the planning process is likely to come about in an ad hoc manner, concentrating on one or another major "problem." It is important to understand problems in terms of their intersectoral, interspatial, and intertemporal contexts. Any regional or local economic development problem can be located in the three dimensions. A problem concerning small shops in the region's major city, for example, might be located in the shaded block in Figure 9.1.

But it is precisely this structure that provides flexibility. Without structure there is amorphousness, not flexibility. For example, one can start with known problems and locate them in the three dimensions, or one can start with the elements of concern in each dimension and define problems in terms of the intersections of these dimensional elements. Starting with the problems, one may discover that it is really a particular sector or level of organizational administration that is of concern. Through this it may be discovered that other problems thought to be separate are in fact related. Similar dynamics take place when starting with the dimensions, because relationships among things are built into the structure.

Suppose funds became available for a program of economic development planning in smaller towns of the region. Where to begin? Which towns? What sort of economic development planning? What data to collect? What analyses to perform? How to link up with other development-planning work in the region? One might start with the shaded slab in Figure 9.1, and make the first step of analytical work an investigation and consideration of the smaller towns in terms of the other two dimensions.

One can aggregate or disaggregate each dimension as appropriate to the situation. One can balance between breadth of scope and depth of scope. The focus can be on the region as a whole but on only one or two sectors, or on all sectors, with less spatial disaggregation. One can start with a 20-year vision or a 2-year vision. Space can be in geographic, topographic, settlement hierarchy, functional hierarchy, urban-rural subspace, jurisdictional, or other terms. Sectors can be in terms of resources, industries, private-public activity, or occupational groups. In some cases a particular enterprise or cooperative or commune may warrant being considered an entire element of a dimension; in some cases a particular town or subarea may be considered an entire element of a dimension. One could even represent the elements of one dimension in terms of the analytical rubrics discussed in Chapter 2 and mentioned again in Chapter 11.

Once principal concerns have been identified in this manner, one has a basis for considering the necessary and appropriate data, analyses, and planning process. If these require resources in excess of those available, the necessary paring back can also readily be determined in the context of the three-dimensional framework. Year after year, with luck, the amount of the framework that is encompassed by analysis and planning grows. Year after year the principal concerns can be redefined. The three-dimensional framework can serve as a basis for defining the focus of limited analysis and planning, for organizing the work, for writing a plan, and for expanding the scope of the effort efficiently, incrementally.

LIMITED PLANNING APPROACHES BASED ON PROJECT EVALUATION

"Limited planning approaches based on project evaluation" refers to choosing among project options without benefit of a strategic framework, but doing it in such a way that a strategic framework can emerge from the project evaluation process itself. This is opposite to the pattern of limited approaches to overall planning. It is not uncommon to come across a case in which assistance for certain types of projects in a region or local area becomes available before the need for them has been articulated through a development-planning process.

For example, through a government or international assistance program, funds might become available for improving local marketplaces in rural areas. Now, it may be known that such marketplaces need improving, so the money will be well spent. But regional plans do not yet exist for the rural areas, so specific local marketplaces that should be improved on a priority basis within the context of well-worked-out regional-development strategies have not yet been identified. Each province or rural region might be required to submit a list of proposed local marketplace improvements that will cost up to a maximum permissible amount of money, if they want to utilize the program. Development practitioners constantly come up against this sort of situation. The question often is, what projects should be implemented so that they best conform to a strategic development framework, when in due course one is formulated? The answer is, project priorities should be based on the likely relative contributions of different potential projects toward achieving what, it is hoped, a strategic development framework would achieve.

Precisely what a strategic development framework should achieve is, of course, a matter to be decided by appropriate means in each case. Suppose that in one region the planning authorities identified the following as the desired achievements of a strategic development framework, when one finally exists:

Development projects that are planned, implemented, and managed efficiently

FIGURE 9.2

Example of a Project Evaluation Framework

Potential Projects to Improve Local Marketplaces in Rural Areas: Project Evaluation Framework	
	Indicators
I. Eligibility Criteria	
A. Is the marketplace of an eligible type?	•Marketplace must serve predominantly the local area, not wholesaling for export from the region.
B. Is the marketplace in a currently eligible location?	•Marketplace must be in a town of 5,000 people or less.
C. Is the project a currently eligible activity?	•Project must be one or a combination of marketplace construction and/or access-road improvements.
D. Is the project within current financial limits?	•Project must cost Mu. 10,000 or less.
II. Preference Criteria	Indicators
A. Planning completeness	•Are plans and specifications completed and cleared by appropriate authorities? •Has an implementation schedule been completed? •Has a management plan been completed?
B. Cost-effectiveness	•What are the project's benefit-cost ratio and internal rate of return: financial, economic, socioeconomic?
C. Contribution to analysis, planning, and development capability	•How many of the following aspects of the project are likely to be repeated often in future projects? Type Technology Location Execution procedures Size Organizational arrangements •In what other way will the project contribute to expanding analysis, planning, and development capability?
D. Promotion of growing prosperity	•When will the project be self-sustaining? •Are the necessary skills available for the long-term management of the project? •Will the project continue to be needed and provide benefits over many years?
E. Equity	•How many and what proportion of the beneficiaries of the project each year are estimated to be poor people?
F. Private sector stimulation	•How much private sector investment will be stimulated by the project in its first five years?
G. Diversification	•In how many of the following ways will the project result in more diversity in the local economy?

144

H. Employment

More types of goods produced   More buyers
More types of goods sold   More market days
More sellers

• How many new permanent jobs will be created: direct, indirect, induced?

I. Natural resource efficiency

• What is the value of alternative uses for the significant natural resources employed?
• What is the natural hazard risk factor?

  1 = no particular risk

  .
  .
  .

  10 = very high risk

J. Regional integration

• How will the project benefit other regional sectors?
• How will the project benefit other subareas of the region?
• Will the project strengthen a regional node?
• How will the project strengthen the overall economy of the region?

K. Participation

• Place an X in the boxes of the matrix below to indicate phases of the project in which participation of groups at different levels is technically possible. Circle those in which the participation has actually taken place or is scheduled. Circled Xs as a percentage of total Xs, the "participation index," is the indicator.

Levels of Participation	Project Phases		
	Identification and Planning	Execution	Management and Operation
Beneficiary groups			
Local leadership			
Local government			
Private sector			
Regional government			
National government			
Others			

145

Development projects that are cost-effective
A growing base of analysis, planning, and development capability
Steadily growing economic prosperity
Equity in the distribution of development benefits
Stimulation of the private sector
Diversity in the local economy
Full employment
Efficient use of natural resources
Regional integration
Broad participation in the planning process

When desired achievements for a strategic regional-development framework like those above are identified, as they usually are through a combination of political and technical means, they can be converted to project evaluation criteria. Such criteria can be divided into eligibility criteria and preference criteria. In other words, minimum standards are set for project eligibility, and additional criteria help sort out from among eligible projects those that are preferable.

Using the examples of desired achievements listed above, development practitioners in a rural region trying to develop a list of priority local marketplace improvements might design a project evaluation framework like that shown in Figure 9.2. Every potential project would first be evaluated in terms of the eligibility criteria. These are firm standards that a project must pass in order to be considered further. Preferences among eligible potential projects are determined through the preference criteria, on a relative basis rather than by absolute standards.

The point of a project evaluation framework like the example in Figure 9.2 is to take into account explicitly what is desired from economic development. By expressing this in terms of explicit criteria and indicators for those criteria, however crudely, the groundwork is laid for an ever-improving strategic framework and the associated data and analysis needed to plan for it. In the case of Figure 9.2, the development practitioners used the eligibility criteria to define the scope of the local marketplace improvement program. Through the indicators they defined the term local marketplace and limited eligible locations, activities, and project sizes to those they believe they can handle competently (for example, they do not yet feel they are ready to handle credit programs for marketplace vendors). The preference criteria reflect the desired achievements, and their indicators reflect the best way currently practicable that the practitioners can think of for gauging contribution toward those achievements.

Again, to some a project evaluation framework like that in Figure 9.2 may seem excessively structured. Again, its aim is indeed to introduce structure. There cannot be collective, equitable, and efficient economic development without ordered decision making; there cannot be flexibility without structure. A strategic development framework will emerge organically as analysis and planning expand over time to support project evaluation based on increasingly refined and well-articulated criteria and their indicators. It might be instructive for the reader to test a familiar local marketplace project—or any regional project, for that matter—against the evaluation framework of Figure 9.2.

Simple as it is, a project evaluation framework like that in Figure 9.2 can be a powerful tool for project evaluation and for expanding regional planning capability, provided, of course, that it is made always to serve decision making, and not the other way around. Criteria may be many or few. Indicators for each criterion may be many or few. If an indicator does not apply to a particular type of project, it can be ignored or changed. Indicators can be in verbal or numeric terms. They can require "best guesses," statistics, or complete analytical methods. Project priorities can be determined by subjective evaluation of the relative performances of potential projects in terms of the preference criteria indicators, or a formal weighting and ranking system can be devised. If the latter, the weights of criteria can be changed as development priorities change. Periodically, a new universe of proposed projects can be evaluated and new priorities set among them. A potential project that turned out a poor preference evaluation in one year can be improved and reevaluated the next year. Criteria can change. Indicators can change and will undoubtedly be increasingly refined as routine information systems and procedures for project evaluation are set in place. The evaluation can be done simply, manually, or it can be expanded to make good use of a computer. The project evaluation framework can be used not only to evaluate a universe of proposed projects, it can be used as well as a basis for identifying and preparing projects. At some point it will become clear that to refine the preference criteria and their indicators to the degree desirable requires undertaking certain methods of regional economic analysis.

MERGING THE TWO

Consider the indicators for preference criterion (j), regional integration, in Figure 9.2. One could choose to replace those indicators with an analysis based on a three-dimensional overall planning framework such as that in Figure 9.1. Or, a new criterion could be established concerning the status of a proposed project within the context of regional-development planning. In between, there are many ways limited approaches to overall planning and limited planning approaches based on project evaluation can be brought closer together. The former focuses on elements of concern in each dimension. The latter focuses on what ultimately will be refined as the goals and objectives of the development effort. It is only natural that if both were done they would soon enough merge as a fairly well-developed analytical and strategic planning framework for the region or local area.

10

COST-BENEFIT
ANALYSIS

From one perspective, the subject of cost-benefit analysis is only remotely connected to the rest of this book. In this chapter the other perspective is taken. It is not just that regional analysts and planners have to be able to work with people whose job it is to do cost-benefit analyses, nor is it just the fact that sooner or later even regional planners have to do a cost-benefit analysis of something. It is, rather, that through familiarity with the concepts of cost-benefit analysis, regional-development practitioners can better express regional issues in cost-benefit terms understandable to others and can ensure that regional implications are incorporated into cost-benefit analyses.

There are three aspects to cost-benefit analysis: deciding what to count as costs and what to count as benefits, deciding how to count them, and calculating the benefit-cost ratio and internal rate of return. They will be presented in order of increasing conceptual complexity, the reverse of the order in which they are listed above.

BENEFIT-COST RATIO AND INTERNAL RATE OF RETURN

Any project can be conceived of as a stream of yearly costs and a stream of yearly benefits over its life. In the simplest case, a project takes one year to build, accounting for all investment costs, and thereafter has annual operating costs and annual benefits as measured by revenues over, say, a 20-year period. A local marketplace from the example in the last chapter could serve as a model. We might want to calculate a benefit-cost ratio to be sure it is above some minimum standard or to compare it with that of an alternate design for the project or with that of an alternate project. And we might want to calculate the internal rate of return to be sure it is above some ac-

TABLE 10.1

Hypothetical Cost–Benefit Data for a Proposed Marketplace:
Streams of Revenues and Costs
(in monetary units)

Year	Revenues (benefits)	Option A		Option B	
		Costs	Net Benefits	Costs	Net Benefits
0	0	1,000	−1,000	0	0
1	300	200	100	420	−120
2	350	200	150	408	−58
3	400	175	225	371	29
4	400	125	275	309	91
5	400	100	300	272	128
6	400	100	300	260	140
7	400	100	300	248	152
8	400	100	300	136	264
9	400	100	300	224	176
10	400	100	300	212	188
11–20	400	100	300	100	300

TABLE 10.2

Hypothetical Cost–Benefit Data for a Proposed Marketplace:
Present Value at Discount Rate of 15 Percent
(in monetary units)

Year	Discount Factor	Revenues (benefits)	Option A		Option B	
			Costs	Net Benefits	Costs	Net Benefits
0	1.000	0	1,000	−1,000	0	0
1	.870	261	174	87	365	−104
2	.756	265	151	114	308	−43
3	.658	263	115	148	244	19
4	.572	229	72	157	177	52
5	.497	199	340	1,022	135	64
[5–20]	[3.404]	[1,362]				
6	.432	173			112	61
7	.376	150			93	57
8	.327	131			44	87
9	.284	114			64	50
10	.247	99			52	47
11–20	1.241	496			124	372
Total		2,380	1,852	528	1,718	662

ceptable standard, or compares favorably with the rate of return on money invested elsewhere, or to compare it with the rate of return on a competing project or an alternate way of financing a project.

Suppose the data for the streams of costs and revenues for a proposed marketplace were as shown in Table 10.1. The revenues are estimated income from the rental of stall space. Rental revenues rise to a constant yearly amount reflecting full occupancy. The construction cost is Mu. 1,000. Operating costs decline to a constant yearly amount reflecting peak efficiency. Under option A the local government pays for the construction out of its current budget and does not amortize the investment. Under option B the construction funds are borrowed at 12 percent per year for ten years.

The figure Mu. 1.00 is worth less next year than it is today. It is worth even less in two years. This expresses itself through the interest rate. If you have a choice between Mu. 1.00 now and Mu. 1.00 next year, you will take it now because, if nothing else, you can invest it and get Mu. 1.00 plus interest next year. This means that even though annual revenue from the rental of marketplace stalls in Table 10.1 is Mu. 400 for years 3-20, each year the Mu. 400 is worth less as we view it from the perspective of today. And the same is true for costs. Thus, the streams of revenues and costs cannot be summed without first converting them into terms of equal values—in particular, into terms of value that make sense in the present, since it is now that the financial commitment must be made.

To convert the streams of future costs and benefits into terms of present value, a rate for discounting future value must be selected. In Table 10.2 a discount rate of 15 percent was used. Although the option B loan had an interest rate of 12 percent, let us suppose that this was through a special central-government program and that on the commercial market investments yield 15 percent. Using a discount rate of 15 percent answers the question, How much would have to be invested today at the market rate of interest of 15 percent in order to yield each of the annual revenue or cost figures in each of the 20 future years? In other words, future values are converted to present values on the assumption that the value of money deteriorates each year in accordance with a 15 percent discount rate.

The present value of an amount A due or available in n years at discount rate r can be computed as

$$\text{Present value} = \frac{A}{(1 + r)^n}$$

In Table 10.1, for example, it can be seen that revenue from the rental of marketplace stalls in the third year will be Mu. 400. Using a discount rate of 15 percent, the present value of that revenue would be

$$\frac{400}{(1 + .15)^3} = \frac{400}{(1.15)^3} = \frac{400}{1.521} = \text{Mu.} 263$$

This is the amount that appears in Table 10.2, in the revenues column for year 3.

Normally, however, the conversion to present value is done with the help of a table entitled "Present Value of One," or "Table of Discount Factors," or something similar. It will be found in any book containing the most basic algebraic tables, including business manuals and high-school algebra textbooks. It will have interest rates along the top and years 0-25 or more along the side. Each box of the table contains a <u>discount factor</u>, the number by which 1.000 should be multiplied to determine its present value for that year and interest rate. If you were to look at the column for 15 percent in such a table, the numbers shown for years 0-10 would be those appearing in Table 10.2. Take the discount factor for year 6, which is 0.432. Investing Mu.0.432 today at 15 percent per year would yield Mu.1.000 in six years. Or, Mu.1.000 in six years is worth Mu.0.432 today. The present value amounts in Table 10.2 were produced by multiplying revenues and costs for each year from Table 10.1 by their respective discount factors.

Mercifully, most projects are estimated to develop a fixed pattern of annual costs and benefits after a period. In Tables 10.1 and 10.2, annual data for option A become fixed starting in year 5. Annual data for option B become fixed starting in year 11. There is a handy formula for dealing with situations like this: (1) sum the discount factors for all the years with constant annual data; then (2) multiply this sum by the constant annual figure. This yields the sum of the present values for all the years with constant annual data. In the case of option A, for example, the sum of discount factors for years 5 through 20 is 3.404. Multiplying 400, 100, and 300 from Table 10.1 in turn by this number yields 1,362, 340, and 1,022 as shown for years 5-20 in Table 10.2.

Once all the data have been converted to present-value terms, the streams of future revenues and costs can be summed. From Table 10.2, the total net benefits, or net present value, and the benefit-cost ratio using a 15 percent discount rate can be seen to be as follows:

	Option A	Option B
Net present value	528	662
Benefit-cost ratio	1.23	1.39

Under option B, with borrowed money, the net present value of the profits from the marketplace over 20 years are higher; for every

Mu. 1. 00 spent, Mu. 1. 39 will be returned at present value, as against Mu. 1. 23 for option A. This makes sense, since under option B the investment cost is spread into future years, diminishing its present value; and the interest rate paid is below the discount rate used.

The internal rate of return is the discount rate at which costs and benefits are equal in present-value terms. In other words, it is the discount rate at which the benefit–cost ratio is 1.00. It is the effective interest earned on the investment in the project.

Table 10.2 showed that the benefit–cost ratio under option A was 1.23, using a discount rate of 15 percent. We are looking for the discount rate at which the benefit–cost ratio is 1.00. It makes sense that this would be a higher discount rate, since a higher rate would further reduce the present value of net benefits in later years, and it is in the later years that the largest net benefits accrue. If we experiment with a discount rate of 25 percent, the benefit–cost ratio under option A will turn out to be 0.93. If we try a discount rate of 24 percent, the benefit–cost ratio will be 0.95. If we try a discount rate of 22 percent, the benefit–cost ratio is 1.03. The internal rate of return, then, is 23 percent. This is rather good performance considering that the rate of return on the commercial market is only 15 percent. The reader may find it a useful exercise to figure the internal rate of return for option B.

As a final step, cost-benefit analysts may undertake a sensitivity analysis. This entails assuming that cost or revenue estimates are inaccurate over some range, say ± 20 percent. The future cost and benefit streams would be independently adjusted up 20 percent and down 20 percent and the impact on the benefit–cost ratio and internal rate of return calculated. The idea here is to see how sensitive cost-benefit analysis ratings of a proposed project are to the range of possible revenue and cost estimation errors. How would options A and B in Table 10.1 work out if actual costs were 20 percent higher than estimated? And what if actual revenues were 20 percent lower than estimated?

Sensitivity analyses might be run on only one component of a cost or benefit stream. For example, under option A it may make sense to assume that construction cost estimates are accurate, and that annual operating costs alone could vary by ± 20 percent.

HOW TO COUNT

Clearly, a great deal turns on the discount rate used. One international lending organization requires that 12 percent be used as the discount rate by all its borrowers when doing a cost-benefit analysis, because as a matter of policy it is prepared to lend for projects with an internal rate of return of 12 percent or better. Put otherwise, the organization is ready to lend for projects with a benefit-cost ratio of 1.00 or better at a discount rate of 12 percent. In some cases it may be appropriate to use the average rate of return on other projects as the discount rate. In some cases the commercial market rate of interest may be appropriate. Often there are a number of discount rates that could legitimately be used, and this is frequently the source of a great deal of debate when proposed projects are being selected and prepared for funding. Of course, it is always possible to run the cost-benefit calculations over a range of discount rates.

For an enterprise intended solely to produce a money profit, costs and benefits are easily counted, as they were in the proposed marketplace example. But suppose in that example the government took a broader view and recognized that other benefits would accrue to the public treasury from the new improved marketplace. As a consequence of increased market activity, a higher volume of business and personal tax revenues would be generated. Or, suppose the government took an even broader view and decided that because the marketplace was meant to be a regional economic development project, the increased market activity, reflecting more production, trade, and income in the area, was itself a benefit. While both tax revenues and market activity can be measured in money, it may not be entirely clear which money to count.

The benefits deriving from the marketplace project should be counted as the estimated additional benefits, the additional tax revenues or market activity, over those without the project. As a general rule, before-after comparisons are made when a project is curative, that is, it is meant to solve an existing problem or improve an existing situation. With-without comparisons are made if a project is preventive, that is, it is meant to prevent an anticipated problem from arising. If the old marketplace that the new one replaced had stabilized at an undesirably low level of activity, the project could be viewed as curative. If the old marketplace were now adequate for local needs but activity showed signs of declining owing to its advancing dilapidation, the project could be viewed as preventive. Yet, one can see that reasonable arguments could be made for a with-without comparison even in the former case; and that the dividing line between curative and preventive can be vague.

There are other counting problems. If a project is to be a public investment, many economists would argue that economic costs rather than just financial costs should be counted. The economic cost refers to counting costs in terms of opportunity costs to the economy rather than actual money paid. The opportunity cost of a thing is the price it would command on the open market in its best alternative use. According to economists, this price represents the value of opportunity foregone, what is given up, in order to use a resource for the proposed project.

Perhaps the two most common situations that cost-benefit analysts run up against where economic costs and financial costs differ are those in which there is high unemployment and/or fixed foreign-exchange rates. In the case of high unemployment, the wages paid to workers constructing the project may be higher than they would earn in other employment, if any could be found. In other words, though the construction workers are paid a certain wage that represents a financial cost to the project, their opportunity cost in terms of the economic benefits foregone owing to their unavailability for other employment are probably much less. To compute the economic cost of the proposed project, shadow prices for construction labor would be estimated representing its opportunity cost. If there are fixed foreign-exchange rates, the shadow price of imported construction materials might be based on the higher black-market foreign-exchange rate, thought to be a better measure of the true value of domestic currency than a rate fixed by the government. If a central-government agency pays duty on imported construction materials, the duty should be deducted from the economic cost, because it is only an interagency transfer rather than an actual expenditure of public resources.

All this has been but a sampling of the counting problems in cost-benefit analysis. The more the perspective on costs and benefits is broadened, the more difficult the counting problem becomes. The easiest case is that in which the project is viewed as a single profit-making enterprise. But economic development projects seldom can be viewed so simply. Because the notion of quantified cost-benefit analysis derives from business planning, and because what is good for a single private business may be bad for private enterprise or the economy collectively, there are frequently situations in which the appropriateness of the conventional cost-benefit analysis approach is arguable. Equally frequent are situations in which the interpretation of the results of a cost-benefit analysis is entirely in dispute.

In the case of the marketplace, for example, it could be argued that the internal rate of return of 23 percent, far from being a good performance, is scandalously high for a public project. Perhaps stall rental fees should be reduced, which would stimulate full occupancy at an earlier date and leave more money in the hands of vendors and others in the private sector, though the benefit-cost ratio might be less than one. Perhaps, through the multiplier, the economic development benefits of such an alternative course of action would be even greater.

WHAT TO COUNT

It is almost impossible to contemplate how to count without touching on the issue of what to count, as was the case in the foregoing discussion. If we estimate conventional shadow prices for construction labor, is this not a statement that we consider the laborers only in terms of their exchange values? One could just as well argue that the economic cost of labor differs from the financial cost of labor because it is a principal purpose of the economy to create jobs, and doing so constitutes a benefit that to some extent offsets costs. We might tabulate reduced public-assistance expenditures, increased personal taxes, and multiplier effects from hiring the construction workers on the project and deduct these from the construction costs.

International lending agencies often wag their fingers at cost-benefit analysts in borrower countries who fail to include the cost of government land in project investment costs. The land belongs to the government, so the government analyst may view it as a free good so far as the public cost of the government project is concerned. But the land has economic value; some measure, like the price it would bring on the open market, represents opportunity forgone, effectively an additional cost, and should be added to other investment costs. It could be argued, however, that to do so is to strive to account for economic efficiency at a level of abstraction so far removed from operating reality as to make it irrelevant to the assessment of a proposed project. Suppose the local analyst knows, as does everyone, that the land is part of a government preserve that, as a matter of policy, will never be for sale. Its market value is zero because it is not in the market. From the perspective of the international lending agency, the policy of the government to withhold its land from the market, or not to value it as if it were on the market, is economically unsound. But is it appropriate to require that the implications of that perspective be imposed on a project cost-benefit analysis that as a practical matter must be viable within a different operational reality?

It should be clear by now that the issue of what to count, as well as how to count, has no absolute resolution. The problem with cost-benefit analysis is that it has an air of authenticity, quantified precision, and objectivity about it that gives it an importance somewhat out of proportion with its technical usefulness. There is no right way and no wrong way to do a cost-benefit analysis, there are only different cost-benefit perspectives. That is why such a simple notion as comparing costs and benefits has spawned such a vast body of literature.

Imagine again the proposed marketplace project. Consider a cost-benefit analysis from the perspective of a private owner; it would probably be similar to Tables 10.1 and 10.2. Now consider it from the perspective of a banker: perhaps the initial investment should be larger under option B to cover operating losses in the first two years. Now consider it from the perspective of the government budget, from the perspective of cost per increment of improvement in the welfare of intended beneficiaries, from the perspective of regional income and product, from the perspective of long-term development dynamics, from the perspective of efficiency in the use of environmental resources, and from the political perspective. Obviously, the rules of analysis differ under each perspective. Or stated otherwise, any set of rules defines a unique perspective. However technical the terms used, the issue is almost always the appropriate cost-benefit perspective. Good project assessment would entail cost-benefit analysis from several perspectives.

To the regional planner, the notion of a regional-development cost-benefit analysis is suggested. The findings of many of the methods of regional economic analysis, especially when available in time series, lend themselves to presentation in a cost-benefit framework. Short of this, many of the tools of regional and local analysis can be used to develop data for conventional types of cost-benefit analysis. In fact, it is through regional and local economic analysis that costs and benefits of potential projects can be linked to broader regional economic development planning.

11

THE GENERAL
PLANNING PROCESS:
FROM GOALS
TO PROJECTS

We all plan. And the basic planning process is the same
whether for personal planning, corporate planning, or regional
planning. The general planning process involves setting goals, ex-
aming options for reaching them, and selecting a course of action.
If planning is done in a dynamic context rather than a controlled one,
it must be a continuing process that incorporates implementation of
a course of action, evaluation, and new information into new cycles
of setting goals, examining options, and so on. Regional or local
development is just such a dynamic context.

What distinguishes one way of planning from another is not the
basic logic of the process, it is rather the way in which the process
is elaborated and the tools that are used for the particular planning
job to be done. In this chapter a general conceptual framework for
regional or local development planning is presented. This is followed
by a review of some basic considerations when using the framework
as a point of departure for designing an actual planning process.

THE GENERAL PLANNING PROCESS

Figure 11.1 is a schematic representation of the general planning
process as it is discussed here. Other models, using different terms
or different numbers of planning steps or a different schematic framework could be equally valid. The scheme in Figure 11.1 has three
special features.

1. Data collection and analysis is not a sequential step in the
process, but a function that continuously supports all others and re-
ceives information from them;

FIGURE 11.1

Schematic Representation of the General Planning Process

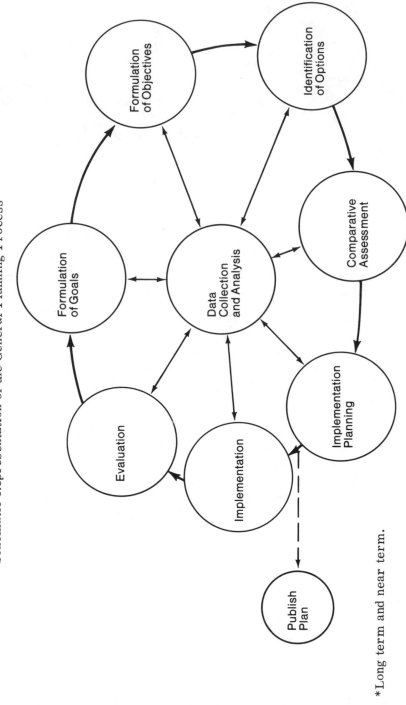

*Long term and near term.

2. All the steps of the process are part of a continuing cycle in which goals are periodically reconsidered, objectives reformulated, and so on;

3. A published plan is not the end of the process or even an integral part of the process, though one may be produced from time to time for a variety of reasons.

The planning support information system can be viewed as encompassing five broad subject areas.

1. Evaluation of the previous planning cycle;

2. The performance of development projects and programs previously undertaken in the area and in similar areas elsewhere;

3. Assessment of development resources external to the area, but available or potentially available to it (public and private funds that might be invested in the interest of local economic development, special talents or capabilities of individuals and institutions that can be tapped, and so on);

4. The characteristics and dynamics of the regional or local setting—including, especially, data on the economy, infrastructure, physical and social characteristics, resources, and institutions;

5. The relationship of the local setting to other areas important to its future development.

Evaluation, the last sequential step in the planning cycle model of Figure 11.1, is an integral component of data collection and analysis. Like other data collection and analysis activities, aspects of evaluation may be going on at all times. It has been shown as a separate step in Figure 11.1 to emphasize the broad evaluative review of the previous planning cycle that should precede a formal goals reformulation. The other four components of the planning support information system speak for themselves. Methods of regional and local economic analysis covered in Chapters 2-7 can be used to good advantage in four of the five subject areas, the exception being assessment of external resources.

It is often useful to establish a set of analytical rubrics to structure data collection and analysis. This subject is fully discussed in Chapter 2. The analytical rubrics selected can carry over from data collection and analysis to the formulation of goals, formulation of objectives, identification of options, and even to the subcommittee organization of those involved in the planning process. This would introduce clarity and consistency along with overall structure into planning process activity.

As argued in an earlier chapter, structure is always welcome in a planning process, for what is planning if not ordered decision making. The proviso is that the structure, such as the set of analytical rubrics, must remain a flexible tool of the planning process and not become a constraining factor. Alternative approaches to structuring analysis and planning will be found in the discussions on limited planning approaches in Chapter 9.

Formulating goals is often given short shrift in regional or local development planning, probably because it is believed that everyone knows what the goals are: expanded employment opportunities, higher incomes, diversification, prosperity, stability, and economic growth. Goals formulated like these really provide very little guidance as to what is desirable or undesirable. Each can be interpreted in many and contradictory ways. Every regional or local development investment should contribute to achieving economic development goals; should represent the best among available alternatives at the time, including a zero investment; should not create side effects inconsistent with community goals; and should not foreclose the possibility of certain future activities that may make a greater contribution to goal achievement. This requires a clear and explicit articulation of development goals.

To be useful for economic development planning purposes, a goal should be able to pass the goal test. The goal test requires positive answers to three questions.

1. Does the goal derive from a future self-image of the community? The self-image should be a long-term one and should relate not only to a static state (for example, more diversified economic activity) but to a local dynamic as well (for example, an increased rate of new enterprise formation).

2. Does it derive from an intimate knowledge of the area based on both quantitative and experiential information?

3. Does it adhere to the what-which rule? A goal for purposes of economic development planning must say what is to be the case with which individuals, organizations, activities, and/or locations, though this should be expressed in nonnumerical terms. It should provide real guidance to the preferable courses of economic development.

The goal test asks nothing more than that a goal be derived from forethought, that it be based on factual information and experience, and that it be specific: "Increase the number of small manufacturing enterprises in the towns of the region," instead of "diversify the economy," for example.

Objectives measure progress toward achievement of goals. They are quantified and time-framed performance targets. Every goal should be expressed in terms of at least one quantified and time-

framed objective. Each can be expressed through more than one objective. In addition to quantified and time-framed objectives, a goal
can be expressed in terms of objectives that are only time-framed;
but in such cases the condition to be achieved within the given time
should be as explicit and clearly discernible as possible. An objective can serve more than one goal.

Initially, an objective may be stated in terms of only the first
increment of time, such as what is to be accomplished toward the
goal in the first two years. There should be both short-term objectives
to be realized during the coming planning cycle, and longer-term
ones. The latter will, of course, be reconsidered in the coming
planning cycle.

If a goal must adhere to the what-which rule, it must be ampli-
fied by at least one objective that adheres to the how much-when
rule. The purposes of economic development activity will thus be
articulated in a set of statements that say clearly how much of what
is supposed to be the case with which individuals, organizations, activities, and/or locations, and by when this should occur. And there
you have the basis for determining the best courses of action.

If a goal is "increase the number of small manufacturing enterprises in the towns of the region," a related objective might be "bring
about the establishment of five new manufacturing firms employing
50 or less in the three largest regional towns within three years."
The number of firms has been quantified for a specific time frame, the
term small has been defined, and priority towns have been identified.
This is indeed a performance target for the planning and development process.

Occasionally, a given objective will suggest a unique course of
action. Occasionally, there will clearly be a limited few options for
achieving a particular objective, and these will readily suggest themselves. But most often there will be a number of relevant options,
many of which will not readily suggest themselves. The aim of the
next step in the planning process is to increase the range of known
options; that is, to identify all potential courses of action that might
contribute to achieving performance targets and, in turn, goals. As
a practical matter, all alternatives can never be identified, but it
reflects the spirit in which this step is taken.

The search is for ideas regarding strategies, projects, and actions that will contribute to the purposes of economic development.
Strategies represent broad approaches, and projects and actions
are specific courses undertaken as the applied expression of a
strategy. Formulation of alternative strategies will coincide with
the identification of alternative projects. Preliminary alternative
strategies may be formulated initially; they are likely to be revised
and new ones formulated as the identification of alternative project

ideas proceeds. Projects proposed independently of each other may be found to have a strategic complementary relationship, which suggests a new strategic alternative that may, in turn, provide a context for identification and consideration of additional project ideas.

Comparative assessment of alternative courses of action can be carried out in many ways. Ultimately, it is perhaps the underlying subject of this book. In a general sense it entails first eliminating strategies and projects that are undesirable, infeasible, or impracticable, and then from the remainder selecting those that are preferred. Chapters 9 and 10 provide some useful notions on this subject. In addition, there is a whole spectrum of assessment-factor checklists, project evaluation systems, comparative assessment matrices, investment priority matrices, and other techniques that can be employed to assist in a comparative assessment. The outcome of this step in the planning process is a package of feasible preferred strategies and major project activity.

Implementation planning can also be thought of as a two-phase step. The task here is to test and refine the package of strategies and projects into specific integrated activities. First a long-term economic development program is prepared that identifies major activities over several years and links them to specific expected results, specific objectives, and through these to specific goals. Then an action plan is prepared covering the next planning cycle or two that details how the first part of the long-term plan is to be carried out. The action plan identifies discrete tasks associated with major activities; and for each it shows when it is to be carried out, the responsible individual or organization, the intended result, the cost, the source of funds, and so on. A formal plan document may or may not be published at this point, but in any case the process moves on to implementation, evaluation, and the next cycle.

The reader may already have protested that the world does not work this way. What has been described is a model, not a prescription. Reality differs indeed, but the function of a model of this sort is to provide an ordered frame of reference as we grapple with that reality. Certainly we may find ourselves starting with projects, jumping to implementation, and then writing a plan. But as we are forced to do these things, a model like this helps us to sow a seed here and there that will contribute to the emergence of a proper planning process.

The reader may also have noticed that even the planning process described here is not so neat and tidy as it might at first appear. It is circles within circles within circles. For example, in the discussion on identification of options, mention was made of a circular interplay between strategies and potential projects. Similar circular interplays, or iterations, take place between the two facets of the comparative assessment step and the two facets of implementation planning. The outcomes of these iterations in turn may cause a rethinking of goals and objectives, and in turn a search for new options, and so on to another level of iterations.

Implementation is naturally going on all the time; project activity cannot stop and wait for the next implementation plan. Elements of evaluation also are always active. So in fact, most of the steps of the planning process are active at all times, and it is only their relative intensities, or perhaps their final determinations for the current planning cycle, that follow a sequential pattern.

The cycles themselves are iterations over a one-to-three-year period. This means that economic development goals may never be achieved, and long-term economic development programs may never be fully implemented. They will be changed long before that. And they should change, because the national environment is changing, the local economy is changing, and people are changing. The function of the long-term goals, objectives, and development program is only to provide a working framework for development decisions in the near term.

REGIONAL CONSIDERATIONS

Using the model as a point of departure, development practitioners can design or redesign a planning process suited to the situation at hand. One of the built-in features of the model described is that it is a learning-based process, which makes it particularly appropriate for development planning, because regional or local development is itself a learning-based process. It is possible to start with a very rudimentary planning process and build up from there as each cycle is succeeded by the next over time.

Following are a few central questions that must receive attention during efforts to design a realistic economic development planning process for a region or local area:

1. What are the interrelationships and interdependencies among development policies as they are formed at different administrative levels and in the private sector? What mechanisms for policy coordination are needed to enable regional development policies to have effect?

2. What are the sources of data and where are the analytical capabilities relevant to different levels of policy formation and decision making? What sort of information system is needed to support the development-planning process? What framework of regional analysis?

3. What instruments of development policy implementation are available at different administrative levels? These instruments include regulation; economic incentives and disincentives; public investment; public procurement; and information, training, and education. What mechanism is needed to unite authority to use these instruments in a manner consistent with the regional or local development planning process?

4. How is coordination among sectors, among places, and over time to be incorporated into the planning process, and through it into the development process?

5. How are aggregative (bottom-up) and disaggregative (top-down) planning to be balanced?

6. How are technical and participatory planning to be balanced?

7. What mechanisms are needed to ensure that the development-planning process remains a learning-based process at all levels?

Regional or local economic development planning is a public, collective decision-making process. It is a proper complement to private decision-making processes. It should be designed and understood as a public decision-making process and not as an exercise apart from that. Those who will be called upon to help implement the decisions must be parties to the decisions. This is not just good ethics, it is good development planning. It is planning that can be effective.

APPENDIX

SOLUTIONS TO
EXERCISES IN PART II

CHAPTER 2

Exercise 3

The rural subspace if rural regions have similar agricultural bases.

The median rural region if rural regions have dissimilar agricultural bases.

The urban region may be appropriate with regard to certain government services.

Rates of change may be compared with national averages in certain cases.

The real issue is, Which are the disparities to be analyzed for local planning purposes and which need to be highlighted for purposes of dealing with higher levels of administration?

CHAPTER 3

Exercise 1

The most obvious questions are

Are all the workers at the factory new immigrants to the region?
Do all the workers at the factory reside in the region?
Is the national average family size appropriate in this case?
Are wages the only form of income generated by the factory?

Beyond this, the analyst has overlooked the multiplier implications of spending by the factory for supplies purchased in the region and regional consumption spending by the workers. There may be additional indirect and induced impacts on the regional economy. More training for the analyst would be a good idea.

Exercise 4

The data in Table A.1 tell quite a story. At a minimum, a number of observations can be made.

The period 19XX–19YY appears to span a considerable amount of time, during which all measures of income as well as population showed substantial growth. Although the proportional growth of the economy considerably exceeded that of the population, the effect on per capita income growth was dampened somewhat by an increased net negative residence adjustment (nonresidents working in the region and taking their earnings out with them), increased transfer payments, and other factors. Nevertheless, regional per capita income showed healthy growth relative to that of the nation as a whole over the period.

While dramatic changes did not take place among the three types of income as proportions of the total, the sources of those earnings changed radically. Nonfarm income tripled and increased as a proportion of the total by over 25 percentage points, an amount roughly equal to the percentage point decline in the proportion of the total represented by agricultural income. The presence of government activity was nominal in 19XX but was a major economic factor by 19YY. The proportion of total income generated by manufacturing roughly doubled over the period to more than 30 percent by 19YY. In short, during the period the character of the region changed from agrarian to government and manufacturing dominated. There was a general diversification of the regional economy and of sources of income over the period, including an increase in the role of property income.

TABLE A.1

Income Accounts for Region Q, 19XX and 19YY
(in thousands of constant monetary units)

	19XX	19YY	Percent Change 19XX-YY	As a Percentage of Total Earnings Paid		
				19XX	19YY	Change 19XX-YY
Earnings by type of payment						
Wages and salaries	650	1,750	169.2	83.9	87.5	+3.6
Other labor income	15	50	233.3	1.9	2.5	+0.6
Proprietors' income	110	200	81.8	14.2	10.0	-4.2
Total earnings by type of payment	775	2,000	158.1	100.0	100.0	
Earnings by industry category						
Farm	425	575	35.3	54.8	28.8	-26.0
Nonfarm	350	1,425	307.1	45.2	71.3	+26.1
Government	35	250	614.3	4.5	12.5	+8.0
Central	30	175		3.9	8.8	+4.9
Civilian	30	100		3.9	5.0	+1.1
Military	0	75		0.0	3.8	+3.8
Local	5	75		0.6	3.8	+3.2
Private nonfarm	315	1,175	273.0	40.6	58.8	+18.2
Manufacturing	110	635	477.3	14.2	31.8	+17.6
Mining	5	5	0.0	0.6	0.3	-0.3
Construction	40	100	150.0	5.1	5.0	-0.1
Communication and transportation	35	80	128.6	4.5	4.0	-0.5
Trade	70	175	150.0	9.0	8.8	-0.2
Finance and related services	20	45	125.0	2.6	2.3	-0.3
Other services and utilities	30	125	316.7	3.9	6.3	+2.4
Other	5	10	100.0	0.6	0.5	-0.1
Total earnings paid by Region Q establishments	775	2,000	158.1	100.0	100.0	
Residence adjustment	(10)	(295)				
Total earnings of Region Q residents	765	1,705				
Property income	75	260				
Transfer payments	20	75				
Less personal contributions to social insurance	(5)	(50)				
Total personal income of Region Q residents	855	1,990				
Population (thousands)	57.5	80.5				
Per capita income (monetary units)	15.0	25.0				
Index (national per capita income = 100)	60.0	85.0				

It might be added that if the period 19XX–19YY does not, in fact, represent the passage of many years, the radical economic change may have created social problems not reflected in the income accounts. There is no indication in the accounts of the distribution of income. Unemployment figures would be helpful in determining whether the income growth benefited all segments of the population or had a polarizing effect. If the greater diversification was accompanied by economic integration, a basis for long-term prosperity may have been created in Region Q. If not, instability may have been introduced that could ultimately offset economic gains with social distress.

CHAPTER 4

Exercise 1

Table A.2 demonstrates one of the many ways the information could be handled. The letters in parentheses key the entries to the information given in the exercise.

Exercise 2

A few of many possible observations might be to

Obtain more information concerning the business sector;
Substitute local products for imported consumer goods;
Reduce leakages to foreign ownership;
Attract debt investment;
Increase reinvestment in the region—that is, stem the flight of capital;
Obtain a more equitable share of tax revenue redistributions.

Region W supplies food to the rest of the country in exchange for manufactured goods, foreign ownership, and central government. Greater diversity would reduce vulnerability to terms of trade fluctuations and would introduce greater stability and growth opportunities. Although the overall balance of payments is positive, the balance-of-payments statement suggests stagnation and vulnerability.

TABLE A.2

Balance-of-Payments Statement, Region W, 19YY
(in monetary units)

Item	Exports and Payments Inflows (+)		Imports and Payments Outflows (-)		Net
Current Account					
Consumer sector					
Farm products					
Cotton	(b)	100,000	(b)		+250,000
Rice	(b)	150,000	(b)		
Manufactured products					
Consumer nondurables	(c)	5,000	(c)	45,000	-90,000
Consumer durables			(e)	50,000	
Services					
Transportation	(f)	7,650	(f)	1,350	-6,700
Tourism and travel	(i)	2,000	(i)	15,000	
Transfers	(j)	25,000	(j)	50,000	-25,000
Business sector					
Capital goods		0		0	0
Supplies		?		?	
Services[a]		?		?	
Transfers, rent, dividends, and so on	(h)	3,000	(g)	78,795	-75,795
Government sector	(m)	15,000			-25,000
Capital goods		?			
Supplies		?			
Services		?			
Transfers			(m)	40,000	
Total					
Capital Account					
Long term			(l)	5,000	-10,000
Short term			(l)	5,000	
Total					
Net Cash Movement[b]					
Errors and Omissions (a)[c]					+17,505

[a] Some travel services included in consumer sector.
[b] Calculated residually, probable error of ± 5 percent.
[c] Not calculated because net cash movements calculated residually.

174

CHAPTER 5

Exercise 3

TABLE A.3

Mix-and-Share Analysis Computations, Region K

	Food Processing	Wood Products	Tourist Crafts	Total
National-Growth Effect (N)				
(1) Regional employment, 19XX	10,000	5,000	3,000	18,000
(2) National growth rate, 19XX-19YY	.07	.07	.07	.07
(3) N = (1) × (2)	+700	+350	+210	+1,260
(4) R = actual regional change, 19XX-19YY	+2,000	+3,000	+1,000	+6,000
(5) Net relative change, R − N = M + S	+1,300	+2,650	+790	+4,740
Industry-Mix Effect (M)				
(1) Percent distribution of national employment, 19XX	0.22	0.67	0.11	1.00
(2) Percent distribution of regional employment, 19XX	0.55	0.28	0.17	1.00
(3) National industry growth rate	+.50	−.17	+.60	+.07
(4) Industry minus national average growth rate	+0.43	−0.24	+0.53	—
(5) Regional employment 19XX	10,000	5,000	3,000	18,000
(6) M = (4) × (5)	+4,300	−1,200	+1,590	+4,690
Regional-Shares Effect (S)				
(1) Regional percent of national total, 19XX	1.00	0.17	0.60	0.40
(2) Regional percent of national total, 19YY	0.80	0.32	0.50	0.50
(3) Change 19XX-19YY = (2) − (1)	−0.20	+0.15	−0.10	+0.10
(4) S = R − N − M	−3,000	+3,850	−800	+50
Employment and Components of Employment Change, Region K				
(1) Employment 19XX	10,000	5,000	3,000	18,000
(2) Employment 19YY	12,000	8,000	4,000	24,000
(3) Change 19XX-19YY	+2,000	+3,000	+1,000	+6,000
(4) National-growth effect (N)	+700	+350	+210	+1,260
(5) Industry-mix effect (M)	+4,300	−1,200	+1,590	+4,690
(6) Regional-shares effect (S)	−3,000	+3,850	−800	+50

CHAPTER 6

Exercise 2

A good guess, though not the only possibility, would be that the region has a relatively diversified nonbasic (use economy) sector and strong basic (exchange economy) industries. It is likely a fairly large region in terms of population, one with a local market large enough to accommodate a diversity of nonbasic activities. Or, it may be a relatively isolated region, so that it would pay to produce most nonbasic goods and services locally rather than import them. Whatever its export industries are, they probably serve the local market as well.

Exercise 3

There is a possibility that the region is part of a country with a centrally planned and administered economy, in which wage rates are not determined by market conditions or influenced by trade unions. If this is not the case, one would expect wages and per capita income to rise. If there are no formal controls, the tendency for per capita income to rise under conditions of growth and a high employment multiplier could be offset by a high degree of foreign ownership leading to massive transfer payments that depress the income multiplier and/or substantial immigration to the region that dampens upward pressures on wages and spreads income over a larger population.

CHAPTER 7

Exercise 1

TABLE A.4

Transactions Table
(in thousands of monetary units)

		Regional Inter-mediate Purchasers				
		Agri-cul-ture	Manu-fac-tur-ing	Ser-vices	Final Pur-chas-ers[a]	Total Out-put
Regional	Agriculture	500	1,130	100	770	2,500
intermediate	Manufacturing	20	120	40	1,320	1,500
suppliers	Services	10	150	90	750	1,000
Primary suppliers (final payments)[a]		1,970	100	770	[b]	2,840
Total inputs		2,500	1,500	1,000	2,840	7,840

[a]Includes households, businesses, government, investment, inventory, and all other export, import, and local final purchasers and primary suppliers.
[b]Sales by primary suppliers to final purchasers are unknown but estimated to be very small.

TABLE A.5

Direct-Requirements Table

		Regional Intermediate Purchasers		
		Agri-culture	Manu-facturing	Services
Regional	Agriculture	0.200	0.753	0.100
intermediate	Manufacturing	0.008	0.080	0.040
suppliers	Services	0.004	0.100	0.090
Primary inputs		0.788	0.067	0.770
Total direct inputs		1.000	1.000	1.000

TABLE A.6

Total-Requirements Computations

	Sales to Final Purchasers	Sales as Direct Inputs				Sales as Indirect Inputs									
						Second Round				Third Round					
		To Agr.	To Mfg.	To Servs.	Total	To Agr.	To Mfg.	To Servs.	Total	To Agr.	To Mfg.	To Servs.	Total	Total	Total Sales
Agriculture															
By agriculture	1.000	.200			.200	(.200)(.200) =.040	(.753)(.008) =.006	(.100)(.004) =.000	.046	(.200)(.046) =.009	(.753)(.003) =.002	(.100)(.002) =.000	.011	.057	1.257
By manufacturing			.008		.008	(.008)(.200) =.002	(.080)(.008) =.001	(.040)(.004) =.000	.003	(.008)(.046) =.000	(.080)(.003) =.000	(.040)(.002) =.000	.000	.003	.011
By services				.004	.004	(.004)(.200) =.001	(.100)(.008) =.001	(.090)(.004) =.000	.002	(.004)(.046) =.000	(.100)(.003) =.000	(.090)(.002) =.000	.000	.002	.006
By primary suppliers					.788	(.788)(.200) =.158	(.067)(.008) =.001	(.770)(.004) =.003	.162	(.788)(.046) =.036	(.067)(.003) =.000	(.770)(.002) =.002	.038	.212	1.000
By all suppliers	1.000				1.000									.274	2.274
Manufacturing															
By agriculture	1.000	.753			.753	(.200)(.753) =.151	(.753)(.080) =.060	(.100)(.100) =.010	.221	(.200)(.221) =.044	(.753)(.016) =.012	(.100)(.020) =.002	.058	.279	1.032
By manufacturing			.080		.080	(.008)(.753) =.006	(.080)(.080) =.006	(.040)(.100) =.004	.016	(.008)(.221) =.002	(.080)(.016) =.001	(.040)(.020) =.001	.004	.020	1.100
By services				.100	.100	(.004)(.753) =.003	(.100)(.080) =.008	(.090)(.100) =.009	.020	(.004)(.221) =.001	(.100)(.016) =.002	(.090)(.020) =.002	.005	.025	.125
By primary suppliers					.067	(.788)(.753) =.593	(.067)(.080) =.005	(.770)(.100) =.077	.675	(.788)(.221) =.174	(.067)(.016) =.001	(.770)(.020) =.015	.190	.933	1.000
By all suppliers	1.000				1.000									1.257	3.257
Services															
By agriculture	1.000	.100			.100	(.200)(.100) =.020	(.753)(.040) =.030	(.100)(.090) =.009	.059	(.200)(.059) =.012	(.753)(.008) =.006	(.100)(.012) =.001	.019	.078	.178
By manufacturing			.040		.040	(.008)(.100) =.001	(.080)(.040) =.003	(.040)(.090) =.004	.008	(.008)(.059) =.000	(.080)(.008) =.001	(.040)(.012) =.000	.001	.009	.049
By services				.090	.090	(.004)(.100) =.000	(.100)(.040) =.004	(.090)(.090) =.008	.012	(.004)(.059) =.000	(.100)(.008) =.001	(.090)(.012) =.001	.002	.014	1.104
By primary suppliers					.770	(.788)(.100) =.079	(.067)(.040) =.003	(.770)(.090) =.069	.151	(.788)(.059) =.046	(.067)(.008) =.001	(.770)(.012) =.009	.056	.230	1.000
By all suppliers	1.000				1.000									.331	2.331

TABLE A. 7

Total-Requirements Table

		Regional Intermediate Industries		
		Agri-culture	Manu-facturing	Services
Regional	Agriculture	1. 257	1. 032	0. 178
intermediate	Manufacturing	0. 011	1. 100	0. 049
inputs	Services	0. 006	0. 125	1. 104
Primary suppliers		1. 000	1. 000	1. 000
Regional		?	?	?
Imports		?	?	?
Total requirements		2. 274	3. 257	2. 331

BIBLIOGRAPHY

THE ECONOMIC AND DEVELOPMENT CONTEXT

City and Region: A Geographical Interpretation, Robert E. Dickinson.
    Humanities Press, New York, 1964.

Development Planning and Spatial Structure, A. Gilbert, ed. John
    Wiley & Sons, London, 1976.

Economics of Location (The), August Losch. Translated from the
    second revised edition by W. H. Woglom, Yale University
    Press, New Haven, Conn., 1954.

Element of Space in Development Planning (The), L. B. M. Mennes,
    J. Tinbergen, and J. G. Waardenburg. Nederlands Economisch
    Instituut, Rotterdam, 1967.

From Peasant to Farmer: A Revolutionary Strategy for Development,
    Raanan Weitz. Columbia University Press, New York, 1971.

Growth Pole Strategy and Regional Development Policy, F. Lo and
    K. Salih, eds. Pergamon Press, Oxford, 1978.

Growth Poles: An Investigation of Their Potential as a Tool for Re-
    gional Economic Development, Vida Nichols. RSRI Discussion
    Paper Series, no. 30, Regional Science Research Institute,
    Philadelphia, 1969.

Growth Poles and Growth Centres as Instruments of Modernization in
    Developing Countries, A Kuklinski, ed. UNRISD/Mouton, The
    Hague, 1972.

Guidelines for Rural Center Planning, Economic and Social Commis-
    sion for Asia and the Pacific. United Nations, New York, 1979.

Introduction to Regional Economics (An), Edgar M. Hoover. Alfred
    A. Knopf, New York, 1971.

Introduction to Regional Science, Walter Isard. Prentice-Hall,
    Englewood Cliffs, N.J., 1975.

Location and Space Economy, Walter Isard. MIT Press and John
     Wiley & Sons, New York, 1956.

Location of Economic Activity (The), Edgar M. Hoover. McGraw-
     Hill, New York, 1948.

Location of Service Towns: An Approach to the Analysis of Central
     Place Systems (The), John U. Marshall. University of Toronto
     Press, Toronto, 1969.

National Growth and Economic Change in the Upper Midwest, James
     M. Henderson, Anne O. Krueger et al. Final report of the
     Upper Midwest Economic Study, University of Minnesota Press,
     Minneapolis, 1965.

Organization of Space in Developing Countries (The), E. A. J. John-
     son. Harvard University Press, Cambridge, Mass., 1970.

Planning a System of Regions, Sergio Boisier. Latin American Insti-
     tute for Economic and Social Planning and the Institute of Social
     Studies, Santiago de Chile, 1981.

Regional Development and Planning, Walter Alonso and John Fried-
     mann, eds. MIT Press, Cambridge, Mass., 1964.

Regional Development Policy: A Case Study of Venezuela, John Fried-
     mann. MIT Press, Cambridge, Mass., 1966.

Regional Economic Growth: Theory and Policy, Horst Siebert. Inter-
     national Textbook, Scranton, Pa., 1969.

Regional Economic Planning, Walter Isard and John H. Cumberland,
     eds. Organization for European Economic Cooperation, Paris,
     1961.

Regional Growth Theory, Harry W. Richardson. Macmillan Press,
     London, 1973.

Regional Planning: A Comprehensive View, Jeremy Alden and Robert
     Morgan. Leonard Hill Books, International Textbook, Heath
     and Reach, United Kingdom, 1974.

Regional Planning: A Systems Approach, J. G. M. Hilhorst. Rotter-
     dam University Press, Rotterdam, 1971.

Regional Policy: Readings in Theory and Applications, John Friedmann and William Alonso. MIT Press, Cambridge, Mass.,
1975.

Regions, Resources, and Economic Growth, Harvey S. Perloff et al.
Johns Hopkins University Press, Baltimore, 1960.

Spatial Organization: The Geographer's View of the World, Ronald
Abler, John S. Adams, and Peter Gould. Prentice-Hall, Engle-
wood Cliffs, N.J., 1971.

Territory and Function, John Friedmann and Clyde Weaver. University of California Press, Berkeley and Los Angeles, 1979.

Urban Functions in Rural Development, Dennis Rondinelli and K.
Ruddle. U.S. Agency for International Development, Washington, D.C., 1976.

METHODS OF REGIONAL ECONOMIC ANALYSIS

Analytical Framework for Regional Development Policy (An), Charles
L. Leven et al. MIT Press, Cambridge, Mass., 1970.

Community Economic Base Study (The), Charles M. Tiebout. Supplementary Paper no. 16, Committee for Economic Development,
New York, 1962.

Design of Regional Accounts, Conference on Regional Accounts, 1959,
Werner Hochwald, ed. Papers presented at the conference,
sponsored by the Committee on Regional Accounts, Johns Hopkins University Press, Baltimore, 1961.

Elements of Input-Output Analysis (The), William H. Miernyk. Ran-
dom House, New York, 1965.

Elements of Regional Accounts, Conference on Regional Accounts,
1962, Werner Z. Hirsch, ed. Papers presented at the confer-

Note: Much of the more useful literature on the methods of regional economic analysis is found in special documents and in journal articles. The reader is encouraged to consult the publications of-
fices of relevant international, professional, public interest, educational, and government organizations, as well as journal indexes.

ence, sponsored by the Committee on Regional Accounts, Johns Hopkins University Press, Baltimore, 1964.

Elements of Regional Economics, Harry W. Richardson. Penguin Books, Harmondsworth, United Kingdom, 1969.

Estimation of Economic Base Multipliers (The), Thomas Hammer. RSRI Discussion Paper Series, no. 22, Regional Science Research Institute, Philadelphia, 1968.

Input–Output and National Accounts, Richard Stone. Organization for European Economic Cooperation, Paris, 1961.

Input–Output and Regional Economics, Harry W. Richardson. Weidenfeld & Nicolson, London, 1972.

Interindustry Economics, Hollis B. Chenery and Paul G. Clark. John Wiley & Sons, New York, 1959.

Local Impact of Foreign Trade: A Study in Methods of Local Economic Accounting, Werner Hochwald et al. National Planning Association, Washington, D. C., 1960.

Methods of Regional Analysis: An Introduction to Regional Science, Walter Isard. MIT Press and John Wiley & Sons, New York, 1960.

Readings in Concepts and Methods of National Income Statistics, George Jaszi et al. U. S. Department of Commerce, Office of Business Economics, Washington, D. C., 1970.

Regional Accounts: Structure and Performance of the New York Region's Economy in the Seventies, Regina Belz Armstrong. Indiana University Press, Bloomington, 1980.

Regional Analysis, L. Needleman, ed. Penguin Books, Harmondsworth, United Kingdom, 1968.

Regional and Interregional Input–Output Analysis: An Annotated Bibliography, Frank Giarratani. West Virginia University Press, Morgantown, 1976.

Regional Economics, Hugh Nourse. McGraw-Hill, New York, 1968.

Regional Income and Product Accounts of North-Eastern Nova Scotia,
Stanislaw Czamanski. Dalhousie University, Institute of Public Affairs, Halifax, Nova Scotia, 1968.

Simulating Regional Economic Development, William H. Miernyk.
Heath-Lexington Books, Lexington, Mass., 1970.

Technique for Area Planning, Regional Economic Development Institute. U.S. Department of Commerce, Economic Development
Administration, Washington, D.C., 1967.

Techniques of Urban Economic Analysis (The), Ralph W. Pfouts, ed.
Chandler-Davis, Trenton, N.J., 1960.

THE PLANNING CONTEXT

Action-Oriented Approaches to Regional Development Planning, Avrom
Bendavid-Val and Peter P. Waller, eds. Praeger, New York,
1975.

Advice and Planning, Martin H. Krieger. Temple University Press,
Philadelphia, 1981.

Analytical Framework for Regional Development Policy (An), C.
Leven et al. MIT Press, Cambridge, Mass., 1970.

Asian Drama: An Inquiry into the Poverty of Nations (an abridgment
by Seth S. King of the Twentieth Century Fund Study), Gunnar
Myrdal. Vintage Books, New York, 1972.

Basic Thinking in Regional Planning, F. B. Gillie. Mouton, The
Hague, 1967.

Case Studies in Information Systems for Regional Development. United
Nations Research Institute for Social Development, Geneva, 1970.

Citizen Participation: Overview and Selected Techniques. University
of Arkansas, Department of Community and Governmental Affairs, Fayetteville, 1981.

Community Participation in Directing Economic Development, Rita
Mae Kelly. Center for Community Economic Development,
Cambridge, Mass., 1976.

Development Planning: Lessons of Experience, Albert Waterston. Johns Hopkins University Press, Baltimore, 1965.

Economic Analysis of Agricultural Projects, J. Price Gittinger. Johns Hopkins University Press, Baltimore, 1982.

Economic Analysis of Projects, Lynn Squire and Herman G. van der Tak. Johns Hopkins University Press, Baltimore, 1975.

Guide to Practical Project Appraisal: Social Cost-Benefit Analysis in Developing Countries, J. Hansen. United Nations Institute for Development Organizations, Vienna, 1978.

Local Economic Development Planning: From Goals to Projects, Avrom Bendavid-Val. Planning Association Series, no. 353, American Planning Association, Chicago, 1980.

Planning Handbook for Communities. Arizona Office of Economic Planning and Development, Phoenix, 1977.

Planning Theory, A. Faludi. Pergamon Press, Oxford, 1973.

Project Appraisal and Planning for Developing Countries, I. M. D. Little and J. A. Mirrlees. Basic Books, New York, 1974.

Public Participation in Planning, W. R. Sewell and J. T. Cappock, eds. John Wiley & Sons, New York, 1977.

Regional Planning and Development: Organization and Strategies, Ann S. Williams and William R. Lassey. Montana State University Press, Bozeman, 1973.

Regional Planning Process (The), David Gilwater and Douglas Hart, eds. Saxon House, Westmead, United Kingdom, 1978.

Retracking America: A Theory of Transactive Planning, John Friedmann. Doubleday, Anchor, New York, 1973.

Shaping Your Community's Economic Future. Oregon Department of Economic Development, Eugene, 1977.

Urban and Regional Development: Policy and Administration, Dennis Rondinelli. Cornell University Press, Ithaca, N.Y., 1975.

Urban and Regional Planning: A Systems Approach, J. B. McLough-
lin. Praeger, New York, 1969.

PERIODICALS

Annals of Regional Science. Bellingham, Wash.: Western Regional
Science Association and Western Washington State University.

Development. Rome: Society for International Development.

Development and Change. The Hague: Institute of Social Studies.

Economic Development and Cultural Change. Chicago: University of
Chicago Press.

Economic Geography. Worcester, Mass.: Clark University.

Ekistics. Reviews on problems and science of human settlements.
Athens: Doxiadis Associates.

Environment and Planning. Leeds, England: University of Leeds.

Growth and Change. Lexington: University of Kentucky.

International Regional Science Review. Urbana: Regional
Science Association and the University of Illinois.

Journal of Regional Science. Philadelphia: Regional Science Research
Institute.

Journal of the American Planning Association. Columbus: Ohio State
University.

Land Economics. Madison: University of Wisconsin Press.

Papers of the Regional Science Association. Urbana: Regional
Science Association and the University of Illinois.

Planning. Chicago: American Planning Association.

Regional Development Dialogue. Nagoya, Japan: United Nations
Centre for Regional Development.

Regional Studies. Tyne, United Kingdom: University of Newcastle.

<u>Socio-Economic Planning Sciences</u>. Stonybrook: State University of
   New York at Stonybrook.

<u>Town Planning Review</u>. Liverpool: University of Liverpool.

INDEX

account: capital, 61; current, 61, 135; income-and-product, 41, 132; social, 129
action plan, 164
advantage: absolute, 3; comparative, 3
agglomeration, 10
aggregative planning, 14
analytical rubrics, 22, 142, 161
assumptions approach, 84, 85

balance-of-payments statement, 52, 135–36
barriers to trade, 4
base multiplier, 82
base ratio, 82, 86, 87, 106; interindustry, 106
basic: regional statistical compendium, 19; sector, 81
before-after comparisons, 154
benefit-cost ratio, 149

capital account, 61
cash movements, 61
column headings, 28–29
commodity flow studies, 56
commodity-flows matrix, 56
comparison: before-after, 154; interareal, 29; intertemporal, 29; norms for, 30; with-without, 154
compendium, 19
compounding of error, 120
constant coefficients, 119
conversion ratio, normative, 83
cost, insurance, and freight (CIF), 59
cost-benefit: analysis, 149; perspectives, 156–57
costs: economic, 154–55; financial, 154–55; opportunity, 154, 155
credit-source studies, 58
criteria: eligibility, 146; preference, 146; project evaluation, 146
curative project, 154
current account, 61, 135
decentralized territorial integration, 14
destination-of-output table, 122
diagonal, major, 113
dimensions, 140
direct: counting techniques, 56; method, 84, 85

direct-requirements: coefficients, 99; table, 96
disaggregation of primary inputs, 114–15
disaggregative planning, 14
discount: factor, 152; rate, 151
discounting, 151
distance, 54; friction of, 54; measure of, 54–55

economic: base, 81, 89; costs, 154; development program, 164
economic-base: analysis, 81; growth trap, 92; study, 83, theory, 81
economics of agglomeration, 10
eligibility criteria, 146
employment, 83; determination, 87
error, compounding of, 120
errors and omissions, 61
evaluation, 161 (see also project evaluation)
exchange economy, 10, 82
expenditures and purchases, 45

final: demand, 96; goods, 35; payments, 96, 102, 108; product, 95; purchasers, 96; purchases, 103, 107; sales, 95; use, 96
final-payments quadrant, 108
final-purchases quadrant, 108
financial costs, 154
flow studies, 56–58
flows, 119
free on board (FOB), 59
friction: of distance, 54; ratio, 54
functional integration, 13
future self-image, 162

general planning process, 159–65
geographic space, 45
goal test, 162
goals, 162
goods flow principle, 59–60
gravity studies, 53–55
gross: margin, 108; national product, 4, 33–34; regional product, 33–34, 35, 37, 132
growth: pole, 10; trap, 92

ABOUT THE AUTHOR

AVROM BENDAVID-VAL holds a master's degree in regional and development economics from the University of Maryland. Since 1966 he has been active as a regional development planner, analyst, researcher, government official, consultant, author, and teacher in Western countries and the developing world. He is a founder and principal of Development Analysis and Programming, Inc., a small consulting firm in Washington, D.C., which specializes in urban and regional development planning and related activities. His other books and monographs include Regional Economic Analysis for Practitioners, Action-Oriented Approaches to Regional Development Planning, Starting Your Own Energy Business, and Local Economic Development Planning. Mr. Bendavid-Val brings to his work an intense concern with strengthening indigenous capacity to plan and manage development activity, a concern amply reflected in the present volume.